The role of the supervising social worker

Alison Davis

Published by
CoramBAAF Adoption and Fostering Academy
41 Brunswick Square
London WC1N 1AZ
www.corambaaf.org.uk

Coram Academy Limited, registered as a company limited by guarantee in England and Wales number 9697712, part of the Coram group, charity number 312278

© Alison Davis, 2022

British Library Cataloguing in Publication Data
A catalogue record for this book is available from the British Library

ISBN 978 1 913384 15 9

Project management by Jo Francis, Publications, CoramBAAF
Designed and typeset by Helen Joubert Design
Printed in Great Britain by The Lavenham Press

All rights reserved. Apart from any fair dealing for the purposes of research or private study, or criticism or review, as permitted under the Copyright, Designs and Patents Act 1988, this publication may not be reproduced, stored in a retrieval system, or transmitted in any form or by any means, without the prior written permission of the publishers.

The moral right of the author has been asserted in accordance with the Copyright, Designs and Patents Act 1988.

 For the latest news on CoramBAAF titles and special offers, sign up to our free publications bulletin at https://corambaaf.org.uk/subscribe.

Contents

1 Introduction — 1
What do we mean by supervision? — 1
How do supervising social workers view their role? — 2
What does this guide cover? — 3

2 Legislative and procedural framework — 4
The early days of fostering — 4
Fostering regulations — 5
National Minimum Standards — 7
The practical implications for supervising social workers — 8
Summary — 10

3 Messages from research and practice — 11
Messages from research — 12
Messages from practice: case reviews — 14
Professional curiosity — 19
Practical application of the lessons learned — 20

4 Establishing the supervision role — 22
Establishing visiting patterns — 22
Supervision agreements — 23
Balancing the need to challenge with the need to provide support — 25
Prioritising and preparing for supervision — 26
Record-keeping practices — 28
Identifying and adapting to foster carers' learning styles — 29
Supervision models — 30
Additional issues to consider — 33
Summary — 37

5 Supporting foster carers to understand their role — 38
Providing inductions — 38
Creating working relationships with foster carers — 41
Providing key information to foster carers — 43
Providing foster carers and their families with support — 50
Summary — 54

6	**Reviews**	**55**
	Why foster carer reviews are needed	55
	Preparing review paperwork	56
	Chairing a review	57
	Supporting foster carers prior to first reviews	58
	The fostering panel	59
	Subsequent reviews	60
	Summary	61
7	**Providing supervision – training and development**	**62**
	Training and development requirements for foster carers	62
	Supervising training and development in practice	64
8	**Providing supervision – case management**	**69**
	Preparing foster carers for a placement of a child	69
	Placement planning meetings	70
	Bridging the gap between foster carers and other professionals	73
	Direct involvement with the child in placement	78
	Supporting foster carers with transitions	79
	Supporting foster carers to manage challenging behaviour	84
	Assisting foster carers to assess outcomes for children	89
9	**Providing supervision – cultural competency**	**91**
	Supporting foster carers looking after young people from different ethnicities	92
	Supporting a young person's cultural identity	94
	Supporting foster carers who are looking after LGBTQ+ young people	96
	Supporting foster carers to address issues of discrimination or bullying	98
	Summary	100
10	**Challenges for supervising social workers**	**101**
	Safeguarding matters	101
	Resistant carers	113
	Flexibility with family and friends carers	114
	Flexible solutions for mainstream carers	116
	Compassion fatigue	116
	Endings and disruptions	119

11 Conclusion	**123**
References	**125**
Appendix 1: Unannounced visit form	**131**
Appendix 2: Compassion satisfaction and compassion fatigue (ProQOL) questionnaire	**133**

Note about the author

Alison Davis qualified as a social worker in 1986 and began her career as a hospital social worker. She then worked for local authorities, where she spent 27 years in a variety of social work roles, ranging from generic social worker to Child Protection and Permanency Planning Chair. She has an MA in Management and has held senior management positions in childcare, children with disability teams, and fostering and adoption.

During her career, she has sat on and chaired both fostering and adoption panels and been an agency decision-maker. She currently works as an independent social worker, chairing two local authority fostering panels, chairing disruption meetings and child appreciation days, and undertaking assessments and investigations, and is an associate trainer for CoramBAAF. She also mentors university students who are considering a career in social work.

Acknowledgements

I would like to extend my gratitude to two fostering teams, the first in Wiltshire Social Care and the second in Pathway Care based in Ashburton, Devon, for making the time to meet and talk with me during a global pandemic when their workloads were high, and they required ingenuity and dedication to continue to support their foster carers. Their contributions were greatly appreciated.

I also need to thank my daughter, Justine, for her advice and encouragement, which ensured I completed this practice guide.

My thanks also go to Jo Francis and her team at CoramBAAF for their skill in the production of the finished article.

Note: The diagrams in this text have been reproduced with the kind permission of their creators (as referenced). In the case of the GROW diagram used in Chapter 5, every effort was made to source permission for use.

Chapter 1
Introduction

The origins of this practice guide stem from the recognition that, while the role of a supervising social worker is unique, complex, and requires a range of social work skills, far more research could, and should, be carried out into it. There are also few dedicated training courses available that can equip social workers with the techniques needed to perform this role effectively.

WHAT DO WE MEAN BY SUPERVISION?

A number of authors have provided definitions of the term "supervision" over the years. Kettle (2015, p 1) stated that 'effective supervision provides a safe space for workers to reflect on their practice, as well as to develop skills and knowledge'. Morrison, writing in *Staff Supervision in Social Care*, defined supervision as 'a process in which one worker is given responsibility to work with another worker in order to meet certain organisational, professional and personal objectives' (1993, p 13).

The Social Work Reform Board (2010, p 13), meanwhile, stated that:

> *Supervision provides a safe environment for critical reflection, challenge and professional support that operates alongside an organisation's appraisal process. It includes time for reflection on practice issues that arise in the course of everyday work, and can help social workers and their managers to do their jobs more effectively. It enables social workers to develop their capacity to use their experiences to review practice, receive feedback on their performance, build emotional resilience and think reflectively about the relationships they have formed with children, adults and families.*

Yvette Stanley, writing about 'Supervision and effective social work practice' in a blog on the Ofsted website in 2018, noted that supervision:

> *…involves talking through the impact the work has on you personally, as well as exploring decision-making. It is vital for practitioners' well-being, professional development, and management oversight. Most importantly, supervision helps you to achieve the best possible outcomes for children.*

Therefore, we can deduce that a supervising social worker works with a foster carer to meet the organisational needs of the fostering service, and the professional and personal needs of the foster carer themself.

HOW DO SUPERVISING SOCIAL WORKERS VIEW THEIR ROLE?

While preparing this practice guide, the author discussed the role of the supervising social worker with staff members at one local authority and one independent fostering service. Although the number of interviews conducted was limited, largely due to the impact of Covid-19 on workloads, the results gained shine a light on the views, feelings and experiences of some of those performing the role.

The interviewees were asked which aspects of the role they enjoyed most, and reported that these were:

- seeing fostered children thrive and develop;
- developing a working relationship with a family;
- working with foster carers who are receptive to new ideas and learning;
- seeing foster families grow and flourish as carers;
- seeing fostered children and families "fall in love";
- watching foster carers provide skilled transitions for fostered children.

The supervising social workers interviewed found that the role was fulfilling and provided them with a range of experiences. As a result, many had remained in the role for a considerable period of time. However, they also noted that it is a challenging role, with the most difficult aspects including:

- managing allegations against carers;
- defining and differentiating between complaints and allegations;
- feeling helpless when watching placements "fall apart";
- balancing the various requirements of the service, such as record-keeping and direct work with foster carers;
- ensuring adherence to the regulations when they conflict with parenting instincts;
- working with foster carers who are avoidant or chaotic;
- building close professional relationships while maintaining boundaries;
- managing their own feelings while dealing with emotive issues;
- working with foster carers who appear to lack empathy;

- helping family and friends carers to understand their changing role as foster carers.

The supervising social workers interviewed all felt that they had received very little training specifically targeted at those performing the role. Whilst acknowledging that there was some training available, for instance, from organisations like CoramBAAF, they all felt that further specialist training would assist them in fulfilling their tasks, which ranged from the very practical aspects of ensuring that equipment and finance were in place to supporting foster carers to offer therapeutic homes for children and advising on complex behavioural issues.

WHAT DOES THIS GUIDE COVER?

Given the messages received from the supervising social workers above, this book was created to provide good practice guidance and recommendations for those who take on this role. It first considers what the role of the supervising social worker entails and how it is defined in legislation. Consideration is then given to the way in which the role came into being and how it has changed over time. The guide examines the small amount of research that has been carried out into the role, and explores case reviews to identify what learning points can be found there regarding this role. The guide then follows the foster carer's journey, through induction, personal development and training, detailing the challenges faced by foster carers relating to the children they care for and the role that the supervising social worker should play in this journey. It examines some of the key aspects of the supervising social worker's role, as well as practice issues identified by those performing it. It is hoped that this guide will assist those undertaking this challenging occupation.

The guide concentrates on legislation in England, although many of the practice recommendations will be valid UK-wide.

Chapter 2
Legislative and procedural framework

This chapter shows how the role of the supervising social worker has evolved over time and discusses some of the key legislation that helped to shape it into the one seen in practice today. This provides insights into the nature of the role, its purpose and the skills it involves.

THE EARLY DAYS OF FOSTERING

While informal fostering has probably occurred for centuries, formal, regulated fostering was only developed in the last century. The introduction of fostering regulations also led to the development of the role of the supervising social worker. This chapter focuses on the changes in legislation and development of regulations that shaped fostering provision and, therefore, the supervision requirements for foster carers.

The history of the role of a supervising social worker can be traced back to a report by Sir William Monckton, which was written for the Home Office in 1945. This referred to concerns relating to the death of a child called Dennis O'Neill, and the care provided to him and his brother who were "boarded out" (the previous term used for "fostered") at a farm. The report highlighted the lack of supervision provided in this placement and led to a call for the better monitoring and supervision of placements of children.

In response, the Government set up two committees to consider the care of children: the Curtis Committee, which examined issues in England and Wales, and the Clyde Committee, which looked at issues in Scotland. Both reports were published in 1946 (Care of Children Committee, 1946; Clyde Committee, 1946).

According to the University of Edinburgh's published timeline of key events in social work (University of Edinburgh, 2017), these reports 'paved the way for the Children Act 1948 (UK)', which established children's departments across the UK. Section 41(1) of this Act stipulated that for 'the purposes of their functions under the enactments specified in subsection (1) of section 39 of this Act, a local authority shall in accordance with the provisions of this section appoint an officer to be known as the Children's Officer', who would receive training and be responsible for the welfare of children in the local authority's care. While the emphasis here was on the role that would, over time, become known as the child's social worker, the concept of focusing on the care that children were receiving in foster placements would eventually lead to the understanding that carers themselves need support and supervision.

Further fostering regulations and legislation were introduced in subsequent years, and these are examined below.

FOSTERING REGULATIONS

Regulations, in this context, are forms of legislation that must be complied with by all fostering services. In the past, fostering was organised under the Boarding-Out of Children Regulations for England and Wales, the first version of which was published in 1955. These regulations focused on visits by childcare officers to inspect homes where children were being cared for to assess childcare and household standards. However, there was limited assessment of the foster carers themselves, and the Act does not mention the provision of any support for or supervision of the carers.

The regulations gradually grew and evolved, with subsequent versions concentrating on improving the care of looked after children. The version of the regulations in place in 1988, for example, looked at the approval of the household, rather than the skills and abilities of the carers themselves. The main requirements were for two references to be obtained for the household, and for conviction checks and personal interviews to be carried out in respect of the applicants. There was no specific requirement for the appointment of a social worker who would support the carers.

The current primary legislation relating to fostering and the role of the supervising social worker is the Children Act 1989. It applies to both local authority fostering services and independent fostering providers, and emphasises that the welfare of the child is paramount. For example, section 2.3 of *The Children Act 1989 Guidance and Regulations Volume 4: Fostering services* includes the following wording:

> *Fostering services must ensure that the welfare, safety and individual needs of looked after children are central to the care provided by foster carers, so that each looked after child is treated as an individual and given personal support tailored to their individual needs and taking their wishes and feelings fully into account.*

The Children Act 1989 and its emphasis on the welfare of the child also led to the publication of the Foster Placement (Children) Regulations 1991, which replaced the Boarding-Out of Children (Foster Placement) Regulations. The 1991 regulations introduced the concept of carrying out more detailed assessments of each carer's ability to meet the needs of the individual children. It also included a requirement for an annual review of carers to be undertaken to ensure that they continue to have the skills and ability to meet children's needs.

Regulations have continued to contribute to the development of both the role of the foster carer, and the role of the fostering service in supervising and supporting the carer. For example, the Care Planning, Placement and Case Review (England) Regulations 2010 (updated 2015 and 2021) focus on placement planning, delegating authority to foster carers, and the independent reviewing of children's care plans. This led to the publication of the Fostering Services (England) Regulations 2011, the set of regulations currently used. Regulation 17(1) of these state, for example, that:

> ...the fostering service provider must provide foster parents with such training, advice, information, and support (including support out of hours), as appears necessary in the interests of the children placed with them.

The Government also issues statutory guidance that clarifies what fostering services must do to comply with the regulations. The current (updated) version of *The Children Act 1989 Guidance and Regulations Volume 4* was published in 2015, for example, and informs fostering services of the steps that they need to take to meet the regulations. These state:

> *5.67 Every foster carer should be allocated an appropriately qualified social worker from the fostering service (the supervising social worker) who is responsible for overseeing the support they receive. It is the supervising social worker's role to supervise the foster carer's work, to ensure that they are meeting the child's needs, and to offer support and a framework to assess the foster carer's performance and develop their skills. They must make regular visits to the foster carer, including at least one unannounced visit a year.*

and

> *5.68 The fostering service should also provide support to the sons and daughters of foster carers and other people living in the foster carer's household who play an important part in supporting children in placement.*

NATIONAL MINIMUM STANDARDS

The concept of National Minimum Standards (NMS) was introduced in the Care Standards Act 2000, which set out the requirements for care standards and inspections for social care. *The Fostering Services: National minimum standards* were subsequently published and last updated in 2011. These set out the minimum requirements for fostering services in England, with an expectation that services will endeavour to exceed these standards. There are separate standards for Wales, the *Statutory Guidance Fostering Services*, relating to Parts 2-16 of the Regulated Fostering Services (Service Providers and Responsible Individuals) (Wales) Regulations 2019. Scotland introduced its own Guidance on the Looked After Children Regulations in 2009 (*National Care Standards: Foster care and family placement services*). However, this guide focuses primarily on the regulations and NMS that apply in England. Supervising social workers should know all of the NMS and be involved in any reviews of the fostering service to confirm that it is meeting the required standards.

The following NMS for fostering services in England are particularly relevant to supervising social workers:

> *21.6) All foster carers have access to adequate social work and other professional support, information, and advice, to enable them to provide consistent, high quality care to the child. This includes assistance with dealing with relevant services, such as health and education. Consideration is given to any help or support needed by the sons and daughters of foster carers.*

> *21.7) The role of the supervising social worker is clear both to the worker and the foster carer.*

> *21.8) Each approved foster carer is supervised by a named, appropriately qualified social worker who has meetings with the foster carer, including at least one unannounced visit a year. Meetings have a clear purpose and provide the opportunity to supervise the foster carer's work, ensure the foster carer is meeting the child's needs, taking into account the child's wishes and feelings, and offer support and a framework to assess the carer's performance and develop their competencies and skills. The frequency of meetings for short break foster carers should be proportionate to the amount of care provided. Foster carers' files include records of supervisory meetings.*

> *21.9) The supervising social worker ensures each foster carer he or she supervises is informed in writing of, and accepts, understands, and operates within, all regulations and standards and with policies and guidance agreed by the fostering service.*

(Department for Education (DfE), 2011, pp 42–43)

THE PRACTICAL IMPLICATIONS FOR SUPERVISING SOCIAL WORKERS

We can see from the information above that the supervising social worker role is identified in both the regulations and the NMS. Indeed, NMS 21.8 (above) spells out the key tasks that a supervising social worker is expected to perform. It is important to note that the NMS, in particular, are used by the Office for Standards in Education, Children's Services and Skills (Ofsted) when carrying out fostering inspections in independent fostering services and childcare inspections in local authorities. Therefore, both individuals and fostering services should regularly review their own performance against these standards.

Providing information to foster carers about regulations and standards

These regulations and standards apply to all fostering services in relation to approved foster carers, including family and friends carers, who are approved for specific child placements. One of a supervising social worker's key roles is to explain the importance of the NMS and regulations to foster carers, so that they understand the standards that the service is required to achieve and the part that they play in helping it to meet these. It may also be helpful for supervising social workers to explain to carers the values that the NMS are based on. These are detailed in the General Introduction of the *Fostering Services: National minimum standards*, and include the following:

The child's welfare, safety and needs are at the centre of their care.

and:

Every child should have their wishes and feelings listened to and taken into account.

and:

Foster carers have a right to full information about the child.

(DfE, 2011, p 3)

Foster carers will understand that these principles are about providing each fostered child with the best opportunities possible, and ensuring that they are valued as an individual.

National Minimum Standards 1–12 (shown below) focus on the children being looked after, and should be shared with foster carers during training or supervision.

> **Child-Focused National Minimum Standards**
>
> Standard 1   Child's wishes and feelings and views of those significant to them.
>
> Standard 2   Promoting a positive identity, potential and valuing diversity through individualised care.
>
> Standard 3   Promoting positive behaviour and relationships.
>
> Standard 4   Protecting from abuse and neglect.
>
> Standard 5   Children missing from care.
>
> Standard 6   Promoting good health and well-being.
>
> Standard 7   Leisure activities.
>
> Standard 8   Promoting educational achievement.
>
> Standard 9   Promoting and supporting contact.
>
> Standard 10   Providing a suitable physical environment for the foster child.
>
> Standard 11   Preparation for placement.
>
> Standard 12   Promoting independence and moves to adulthood and leaving care.
>
> (DfE, 2011)

The NMS emphasise how fostering should be aspirational for children. For example, according to NMS 3.1, foster carers should 'have high expectations of all of the foster children in their household' (DfE, 2011, p 12). Additionally, NMS 8.4 states that children should be 'helped by their foster carer to achieve their educational or training goals' (DfE, 2011, p 20).

Registration, experience and knowledge

Those performing the supervising social worker role must be registered with their professional regulator (for example, Social Work England). It is advantageous if they have childcare social work experience and can use this knowledge to explain the relevant policies, procedures and working practices to the carers whom they support.

NMS 23.5 states that the 'assessment and appraisal of all staff involved in fostering work' should take account 'of identified skills needed for particular roles' (DfE, 2011, p 47). NMS 23.1, meanwhile, requires each service to have a good quality learning and development programme for staff, that 'equips them with the skills required to meet the needs of children, keeps them up to date with professional, legal and practice developments and reflects the policies, legal obligations and business needs of the fostering service' (DfE, 2011, p 47). The NMS do not specify which skills and knowledge are needed for staff in a fostering service, but the supervising social worker role requires skills such as:

- Understanding of child development
- Understanding of the impact of trauma and loss on child development
- Understanding of attachment
- Knowledge of anti-discriminatory practice
- Knowledge of behaviour management
- Knowledge of therapeutic parenting
- Knowledge of safeguarding
- Knowledge of childcare planning
- Knowledge of adult learning styles
- Supervision skills
- Ability to mentor and coach
- Ability to encourage reflective practice
- Mediation skills
- Good communications skills and the ability to work collaboratively
- Ability to challenge constructively
- Ability to produce SMART action plans
- Ability to analyse situations and produce evidence-based reports

These will be discussed further in subsequent chapters.

SUMMARY

All supervising social workers need to know and thoroughly understand fostering standards and regulations so that they can support their foster carers appropriately. However, viewing these standards and regulations in the context of the historical development of the role will enable supervising social workers to gain greater insight into the reasoning behind them and may, therefore, enable them to supervise their carers more effectively. However, it is also important for them to broaden their knowledge and understanding by considering learning from research and case reviews. We examine the benefits of this in the next chapter.

Chapter 3
Messages from research and practice

This chapter examines the research that has been undertaken into the role of the supervising social worker, highlighting key studies that would be of value for social workers to consider in more detail. It shows the dichotomy between foster carers' concepts of what the supervising social worker role entails, and the requirements as set out in the legislation and standards. It also details a number of recent case reviews that have particular significance for those fulfilling the supervising social worker role.

In September 2014, the University of Oxford's Rees Centre for Research in Fostering and Education published an international literature review, titled *The Role of the Supervising Social Worker in Foster Care* (Cosis Brown *et al*). In this report, the authors highlighted that this role is a 'relatively recent development' (p 7), and is 'complex since it encompasses both the support and supervisory aspects of work done with the foster carer' (p 4). They observed that the majority of research undertaken to date had viewed the role of a supervising social worker 'from the foster carers' perspective with relatively little attention given to the perceptions of the supervisory social workers or the fostering providers' (p 5).

Four years later, in a journal paper titled 'The supervising social worker in the inner city', Jaggar also noted that there had been a 'noticeable lack of research into the values, perspectives and experiences of supervising social workers' (2018, p 384).

Despite this, however, supervising social workers can take something from the existing studies that trace the development, requirements and challenges of the role. They can also learn much from considering case reviews. This chapter details some of the messages that can be found in material published to date.

MESSAGES FROM RESEARCH

The nature of the supervising social worker role

The role of a separate social worker to support foster carers has developed over time, and has been discussed in a number of publications. In the 1980s, it was not unusual for social workers to have a generic caseload that included providing support to a few foster carers. However, during the 1990s, supporting carers became a more specific task for fostering social workers. Writing in 1999, for example, Sellick notes that 'family placement social workers have various titles, ranging from the rather dated "fostering officer" to the somewhat incomplete "homefinder", a title that refers to recruitment and assessment tasks but implies that support and retention tasks are less important' (Sellick, 1996, p 240). Sellick uses the term "link social worker" in his article, as he feels that 'it sums up the whole range of work with foster carers, children and their relatives and with the social workers of children and their families' (Sellick, 1996, p 240).

This role was often seen as one of support rather than supervision. In a journal paper titled 'Recruiting and retaining foster carers: implications for professional practice in Fife', Ramsay states:

> *Each foster home has a link social worker, normally the worker who carried out their assessment. The link worker's main tasks are to ensure the carers' training and practical needs are met; to offer ongoing support and guidance; and to ensure placement contracts are drawn up which meet the needs of both child and carer.*

(1996, pp 42–46)

The challenges faced by supervising social workers

The development of NMS and measurable childcare practices, together with the requirements of modern childcare social work, including the use of electronic recording systems, has led to greater emphasis being placed on the supervision of foster carers as part of a national ambition to raise the quality of childcare provision. This is reflected in the most recent title for the role. This can sometimes lead to tensions, both for supervising social workers and their relationships with foster carers, who may have differing perceptions of the role. Jaggar (2018) referred to findings in a focus group of supervising social workers which described a conflict between 'care and control' (p 394).

It is noticeable that when foster carers are asked what they require from a supervising social worker, they focus on the support aspects of the role rather than the supervisory processes. Cosis Brown *et al* (2014) reviewed 24 research publications and concluded that the foster carers valued the following aspects of social work provision: emotional support; availability and reliability; home visits; support in relation to contact; support at times of crisis; and provision of respite (p 13). They did not highlight the contribution made by the supervising social worker to their personal development or the requirement to ensure that their home and child care met defined standards, both of which form part of the supervisory role.

This could suggest that the supervising social worker faces an ongoing challenge in terms of providing the support that the foster carer needs and values, whilst also meeting the requirements of the law, the NMS, and the requirements of their fostering service.

What foster carers want from a supervising social worker

In their 2013 journal paper, 'Should I stay, or should I go? A mixed methods study examining the factors influencing foster parents' decisions to continue or discontinue providing foster care', Geiger *et al* found that when 'foster parents are receiving the social, emotional, financial and practical supports they require and feel as though their thoughts and voices are being heard, the satisfaction they experience can be enhanced' (p 1365).

The Research in Practice group expanded on this in their Key Messages Topic 7, *Leadership and Supervision*, on supervising foster carers, stating that:

> *...satisfaction amongst foster carers is highest when:*

- *foster carers received monthly social worker visits that last longer than an hour*

- *there is effective teamwork and communication, and foster carers have confidence in agency professionals*

- *professionals provide recognition, respect and encouragement to foster carers for their dedication and efforts*

- *foster carers are heard and included in discussions about the child (Geiger et al, 2013).*

(Research in Practice, 2014)

This suggests that foster carers value supervising social workers who give them time, enable them to feel part of the team around the child, hear their contributions, and value them.

Sinclair *et al* (2004, p 171) stated that foster carers:

> *...need support that respects their family contexts, their commitment and their skill. They need efficient handling of their practical issues and a sympathetic response to their emergencies. Their support requires money, training and clarity of policy and procedure.*

This is echoed by Lorna Miles in *Holding On and Hanging In* (2010). Lorna, a foster carer, describes how much she appreciated her supervising social worker who, whilst being skilled in family therapy, was also practical in her parenting advice. She valued the fact that, no matter how busy the supervising social worker was, she always responded to the family's phone messages, even if it was only to say that she would contact them for a discussion later. This made the family feel less isolated when they were experiencing a difficulty with a fostered young person, and reinforced the fact that they were part of a team. In a recent conversation, Lorna also noted that when there was an issue in the foster home, the supervising social worker would often just "pop in" to see how things were going, which was much appreciated (Miles, personal communication, May 2020).

This reflects Sinclair *et al*'s (2004) findings. Their survey relating to the frequency of contact between supervising social workers and foster carers showed that there was a strong association between the frequency of phone contact and the likelihood of carers continuing to foster (p 136).

There is recent evidence that foster carers generally feel well supported by their supervising social workers. Lawson and Cann, in their 2019 report, *The State of the Nation's Foster Care*, found that 70 per cent of foster carers felt the support they received from their supervising social worker was either "excellent" or "good" (p 13).

MESSAGES FROM PRACTICE: CASE REVIEWS

The term "case reviews" is used in the discussion that follows, as this was the correct terminology when most of the reviews discussed here were published. However, since June 2018, following the publishing of the Children and Social Work Act 2017, these are now called child safeguarding practice reviews.

In the absence of substantial research and literature focusing on the role of the supervising social worker, there are significant learning points within recent case reviews. While these could be described as being on the extreme end of a spectrum of learning opportunities for supervising social workers, as they relate to cases where children in foster care have been seriously harmed, they highlight key practice issues. Below are some examples of case reviews in which the supervising social worker played a key part.

Case Review 1: City and Hackney Safeguarding Children Board (Ibbetson, 2014)

A case review undertaken by City and Hackney Safeguarding Children Board in 2014 considered a case in which a number of children had been sexually abused by a foster carer and one of his family members. Although the abuse happened between 1999 and 2008, the offences did not come to light until a much later date. In section 1.28 of the Overview Report, the author expresses concerns that the fostering service staff had developed 'an uncritical and unhealthy relationship with the foster carers' (Ibbetson, 2014, p 6). They note that the carers were initially seen as 'being flexible, child centred and happy to assist the local authority' (p 6). In section 3.8 of the report, they add that the carers 'would accept placements of children with a range of needs and were co-operative when children had to be placed quickly. They were perceived as having worked in a very open way with birth parents' (p 14). Over time, the foster carers gained a reputation for being able to offer placements to more challenging children.

When concerns were eventually raised, initially about the standards of care that the foster carers were providing and later about the possibility that children within their care had been sexually abused, it was felt that the fostering service minimised these.

According to section 1.31 of the report, the couple 'operated outside of the normal rules and procedures of the fostering service by, for example, refusing to attend training or supervision sessions', and were 'openly hostile to some professionals' (p 7). The report's author notes that the female foster carer treated one supervising social worker, who began to make unannounced visits after becoming concerned about the fostered children within the home, in a particularly hostile way and made a number of informal complaints about her (p 48). However, the case review concluded that the foster carers were not challenged because the fostering service held them in high esteem. The case review considered that the foster carers' behaviour could be described as the '"grooming" or "conditioning" of the professional network', and noted that the carers engaged in this behaviour in an attempt to 'cultivate a favourable impression among professionals and to deflect or dampen any criticism' of the care that they were providing (p 7).

Case Review 2: Southampton Safeguarding Children Board (Wonnacott, 2018)

The same themes were echoed in a case review commissioned by Southampton Safeguarding Board. This considered allegations against foster carers and abuse of children in care. It primarily focused on two individual foster carers who were either convicted of, or being investigated for, child abuse incidents that took place between January 1994 and September 2013. The review concluded that:

- the carers 'were seen as a useful resource as they were willing to look after children whose behaviour was deemed to be challenging' (Wonnacott, 2018, p 16);

- when challenged themselves, the carers made complaints or threatened to end placements;

- defaults were noticed by the fostering services and recorded, but no actions seemed to have been taken to address them;

- patterns of concerns were not identified and addressed; and

- the 'focus was on supporting foster carers rather than challenging their behaviour' (p 17).

Case Review 3: NSPCC, Young Person F, 2018/C7320 (Unnamed Local Safeguarding Board, 2018)

In 2018, the NSPCC published a case review by an unnamed Local Safeguarding Board about Young Person F, who appeared to be failing to thrive in foster care. The review covered the seven-year period to November 2015 and looked at the care he was receiving from his foster carers, who were receiving 'a comprehensive package of support', but who still stated that they felt unsupported (p 2). The case review noted that the foster carers made complaints about professionals to the extent that, in 2008, the child's social worker asked for the case to be re-allocated (p 2), and that one of the carers was considered to be manipulating professionals by forming 'alliances' that excluded others in the professional network so the focus on the child was reduced (p 12). The case review stated that the 'supervision of foster carers was not effective in that there was not sufficient challenge from the supervising social workers in relation to concerns about their care, with the relationship between foster carers and their fostering social workers becoming uncritical' (p 12).

Case Review 4: Trafford Safeguarding Children Board (2017)

In 2017, Trafford Safeguarding Children Board published a case review in respect of Child PB's foster placements. He was accommodated at the age of 12 and placed in two consecutive placements with single carers. He later alleged that sexual abuse had taken place in both households. Foster Carer 1 regularly referred to his own ill health during PB's placement, and eventually ended the placement because of this (Trafford Safeguarding Children Board, 2017, p 18). However, the case review noted that he had never been 'asked by his supervising social worker to undergo a medical examination to confirm his fitness to foster and a short time later, he advised he was feeling much better and agreed to a respite placement for another young person' (p 18). During these placements, there were concerns that Foster Carer 1 was 'not reporting significant events, not following procedures and disagreeing with safe practice requests from the supervising social worker' (p 18). However, the report notes that the issues were not looked at holistically 'and did not lead, as they should have done, to a review' of the foster carer (p 18).

Prior to PB's second placement, with Foster Carer 2, an unsubstantiated allegation had been made that Foster Carer 2 had provided two young people with alcohol (p 18). While Foster Carer 2 was looking after PB, concerns were raised about 'his ability to manage behaviour' and sleeping arrangements within the home (p 18). Furthermore, once PB had moved to a residential placement, Foster Carer 2 was found to be providing shelter for PB when he absconded (p 18).

The case review found that the patterns of behaviour of the two foster carers had not been analysed and challenged, and there was evidence of 'disguised compliance' (p 19) from both of them.

Case Review 5: NSPCC, Child F, 2019/C7931 (Hawkins, 2019)

In 2019, the NSPCC published an overview report of Child F, which involved an unnamed Local Safeguarding Children Board. Child F, who had been in foster care following a traumatic childhood, was 'an immensely private child' who 'did not want other young people to know about their looked after status', so everything about the case was anonymised in order to respect this (Hawkins, 2019, p 4).

Child F had been complaining of feeling ill, listing a number of symptoms at various times, including having stomach pains, feeling dizzy, feeling nauseated, and vomiting. However, their foster carers and professionals felt that this was related to the child's past experiences. For example, the report notes that, on one occasion, the foster carers stated that 'they thought that Child F was using physical health as a reason not to have difficult conversations' (p 15). Child F 'was not eating with the family', but the foster carers believed that they were buying junk food and eating that instead (p 15).

Child F 'advised the social worker that they had concerns regarding the quality of care being given by the foster carer' (p 16). This information was passed on to the supervising social worker, who visited and spoke with Child F. According to the case review, whilst the supervising social worker did then speak with the foster carers, an Independent Managed Review (IMR) produced by Children's Social Care found that the supervising social worker's discussions with both the child and the foster carers appeared to reinforce the view that Child F's issues were psychological in origin (p 17). Child F was later moved from the placement at the request of the foster carers and placed with a respite carer (p 18). During this placement, the child was referred to a GP, who noticed that they were walking with an unusual gait and referred them to hospital (p 20). They were found to have a brain tumour and eventually died as a result of the condition (p 20).

The case review found that the 'supervision of the foster carers was not sufficiently challenging and neither the social worker nor supervising social worker challenged the picture being presented' (p 29). Recommendation 5 of the report states that lessons 'from this review should be incorporated into foster carer recruitment, training and supervision, by Children's Social Care. This should be audited by the LSCB to ensure compliance' (p 32).

Case Review 6: Warwickshire Safeguarding Children Board (Bentley-Lawson, 2017)

A redacted report based on a case review in respect of Child T, published by Warwickshire Safeguarding Children Board in 2017, discussed the death of a 23-month-old child. Child T died in foster care and his foster mother subsequently pleaded guilty to manslaughter.

The case review considered the visiting pattern to this household. Whilst the NMS do not specify the frequency with which visits should be undertaken to a foster carer, this is a matter for both the fostering service and the supervising social worker. They should take into account the current issues under consideration for the child or young person placed, and their decision should be based on an assessment of the fostering household and its needs.

The review of Child T considered that, apart from during a 10-month period when they did not have a supervising social worker, the foster family had been visited within the guidelines set out by Warwickshire County Council: at intervals of a minimum of four months, and with one unannounced visit per year and an annual review (Bentley-Lawson, 2017, pp 15–16). These visits were recorded, but 'there was a lack of critical appraisal' of the foster carers' skills (p 18), and a lack of focus on the safeguarding and well-being of the child placed (p 17). The case review also notes that although 'one unannounced visit took place in July 2011', it 'would have been insufficient to gain an insight as to how the couple were functioning as foster carers' (p 16).

Additionally, the case review noted that the social workers did not recognise that the foster carers had 'gaps' in their 'knowledge of child development and attachment theory', which led to unrealistic expectations of the child (p 19). The author added that: 'the need to robustly challenge such views and to ensure that suitable training is made available to and taken up by foster carers is an important finding of this review' (p 19).

MESSAGES FROM RESEARCH AND PRACTICE

What can supervising social workers learn from these case reviews?

Some key points arising from these case reviews are set out below.

- Supervising social workers need to maintain a professional distance from foster carers to enable critical analysis of their actions (Case Review 1, City and Hackney, and Case Review 6, Warwickshire).

- Supervising social workers need to challenge foster carers who fail to meet minimum standards or to engage with service requirements, such as training, recording, etc, or who make regular complaints about professionals (Case Review 1, City and Hackney; Case Review 2, Southampton; and Case Review 3, NSPCC).

- Supervising social workers should note and address patterns of concern that arise (Case Review 2, Southampton, and Case Review 4, Trafford).

- Medical information self-reported by a foster carer or provided as their assessment of a child's condition should be verified by a medical adviser (Case Review 4, Trafford, and Case Review 5, NSPCC).

- Supervising social workers should ensure that supervision sessions with foster carers include appropriate challenge (Case Review 4, Trafford; Case Review 5, NSPCC; and Case Review 6, Warwickshire).

PROFESSIONAL CURIOSITY

All of the above key points require the use of professional curiosity. This enables a deeper understanding of foster carers and their households.

What Is professional curiosity?

In a bulletin published in 2017, titled *Working Together to Improve Professional Curiosity*, Brighton and Hove Local Safeguarding Board defines professional curiosity as 'the capacity and communication skill to explore and understand what is happening within a family rather than making assumptions or accepting things at face value'.

It notes that the social worker should 'ask questions and seek' clarity if they are unsure about issues, be prepared to review their assessments if information emerges that does not support an initial hypothesis, and always 'be open to the unexpected'.

(Brighton and Hove Local Safeguarding Board, 2017, p 1)

Curiosity and reflection are skills that childcare social workers use regularly in child protection investigations with families. However, they should also be used by supervising social workers with the foster families whom they support. In particular, professional curiosity means not relying on self-reporting alone, but identifying evidence to support statements. This is particularly noticeable in Case Review 4 (Trafford), where the foster carer reported ill health during the placement and provided this as his reason for ending it. The supervising social worker did not seem to explore these medical issues or investigate how they had been resolved so that the foster carer could take another placement within a short timescale.

> **Professional curiosity – the NSPCC's view**
>
> The NSPCC referred to professional curiosity in January 2020, when it examined case reviews relating to cases of child sexual abuse that had been published from 2017 onwards. It highlighted the need for professionals to be 'continually challenging and curious', and the importance of 'continually monitoring the care the child is receiving' from foster carers throughout their placement.
>
> (NSPCC, 2020, p 2 and p 5).

PRACTICAL APPLICATION OF THE LESSONS LEARNED

So how can a supervising social worker ensure that they are aware of and alert to the issues raised in the literature, research and case reviews, and incorporate what they have learned into their practice?

They can:

- ensure that foster carers understand that a supervising social worker's role is both to supervise and support;
- make regular visits to the foster carer and emphasise the importance of foster carers attending training;
- respond to the foster carer in a timely manner;
- provide additional support at times of stress or crisis;
- ensure that the foster carer feels part of the professional team and valued;
- challenge inappropriate actions or concerns;

- ask "curious questions";
- keep up to date by reading newly published case reviews;
- complete training on professional curiosity, disguised compliance and critical analysis;
- ensure that their safeguarding training is up to date;
- be prepared to challenge attitudes and behaviour that are not in line with NMS and service expectations;
- maintain a chronology of issues and identify patterns of concern;
- use their own supervision sessions to discuss and explore their understanding of the fostering household, and challenge and review any hypotheses.

However, in order to undertake the above tasks successfully, they must first establish a supervisory relationship with their foster carers. In the next chapter, we consider how they can undertake this in an effective way.

Chapter 4
Establishing the supervision role

This chapter expands on the concept of supervision first presented in Chapter 1. It examines how supervision is established in practice, considers the different mix of support and challenge that can be present in a supervisory relationship, and discusses various supervision models. It also considers how both the foster carer's and the supervising social worker's learning styles can impact on the outcomes of a supervisory relationship.

ESTABLISHING VISITING PATTERNS

The regulations require supervising social workers to visit foster carers on a regular basis. Usually, these visits occur every month or six weeks. Most agencies consider it good practice to visit every month, and this helps to build the working relationship between the supervising social worker and foster family. In the first year after approval, the supervising social worker should consider visiting more frequently, as foster carers may have many questions about policies, procedures and practice issues, and may require help to complete the Training, Support and Development (TSD) standards workbook. They may also need additional support from the supervising social worker during their first few placements. Some supervising social workers phone all of their foster carers every week, whether each carer feels that they have anything they wish to discuss or not. By doing this, the supervising social worker establishes clear lines of communication, and foster carers have the opportunity to ask questions about minor issues that they might not feel are significant enough to warrant a phone call to the worker.

Following the publication of the Care Planning and Fostering (Miscellaneous Amendments) (England) Regulations 2015, young people who have been in long-term matched placements for more than 12 months may have less frequent visits from the child's social worker. However, the frequency of these visits can be increased at times of stress within the foster home, or decreased if the children are in stable, long-term placements. Similarly, supervising social workers should vary the frequency of their visits according to the needs of the fostering household. Where foster carers are offering specialist therapeutic or assessment placements, such as parent and child placements, visits are often much more frequent according to the complexity of the situation that the foster carer is managing. Adams and Dibben (2020) discuss this subject in greater detail.

NMS 21.8 stipulates that the 'frequency of meetings for short break foster carers should be proportionate to the amount of care provided'. Each fostering service needs to agree what "proportionate" visiting actually means for their short break foster carers. Many short break carers only offer weekend respite for one or two weekends a month. In such cases, it could be argued that a truly proportionate response would be for the supervising social worker to visit them once or twice a year. However, this would not allow them enough time to review placements, to ensure that the carers' training is up to date, to help the carers to develop their skills, and to undertake health and safety assessments. Therefore, many services undertake supervisory visits to short break carers every two–three months. If this occurs, good practice would be for the foster carers to receive phone calls from their supervisors on the months they do not visit. This will ensure that carers have the opportunity to raise any issues that they have before these develop into more serious concerns.

The supervising social worker should also give additional thought to situations where two foster carers are involved. Will both carers be present at all supervisory visits, for example, or will the primary foster carer attend all sessions while the secondary foster carer attends a minimum number of sessions each year? Where the secondary foster carer works long hours or is away from the family home for extended periods of time, the supervising social worker could arrange phone sessions or use online video facilities such as Skype, FaceTime or Zoom, so that they are fully involved with the fostering service.

Whatever visiting pattern is established, the supervising social worker should always update the carers about any changes that have been made to legislation, regulations and standards, or to service policies, during these visits. They should also explain the impact that these changes may have on the foster carers and the children for whom they are caring.

SUPERVISION AGREEMENTS

Supervising social workers can ensure that their working relationship with a foster carer is built on a solid foundation, by defining this relationship with a clear supervision agreement.

The key elements of supervision for foster carers and supervising social workers

Supervision should allow foster carers to:

- talk about the impact that fostering and the child currently placed are having on them;

- reflect on the therapeutic care needs of the child they are looking after and discuss how best they can meet the needs of each individual;

- reflect on how trauma and loss may have impacted on the child's behaviour and think about their attachment needs;

- reflect on the voice of the child placed with them;

- inform their caregiving by "putting themselves in the shoes of the child";

- reflect on the service that they are providing;

- begin to build emotional resilience;

- reflect on the relationships that they and other household members are forming with the child;

- ensure that the daily decisions they make for the child are understood and supported by the fostering service;

- further develop their fostering knowledge and skills;

- receive feedback on their performance;

- raise any concerns or questions they may have about the plans for the child; and

- ensure that their practical needs are being heard.

Supervision should enable the supervising social worker to:

- understand the current relationships and issues within the fostering household;

- understand the child's therapeutic care needs by reflecting with the carer about how the child presents and how they respond to care offered by the carer;

- understand the current emotional impact that fostering is having on the carer and their immediate family;

- discuss the current plans for any foster child placed with the carer and the carer's understanding of these plans;

- consider the carer's ability to meet the professional requirements to be a foster carer, including their participation in supervision and training, and their record-keeping competency;
- assess whether or not the foster carer is able to translate learning and development into practice;
- identify any learning needs;
- check that the child in placement is safeguarded at all times;
- update the carer on any changes and developments that are taking place within the fostering service;
- ensure that the foster carer is informed about new legal or regulatory developments;
- establish whether there is a need to be a "bridge" between the foster carer and other professionals.

BALANCING THE NEED TO CHALLENGE WITH THE NEED TO PROVIDE SUPPORT

Clearly, the supervising social worker needs to provide support to the carer and to challenge them, and they must balance these requirements properly. The diagram below shows the potential mixes of support and challenge, and the impact that taking each approach can have on the supervisory relationship.

Figure 1: Mixes of support and challenge

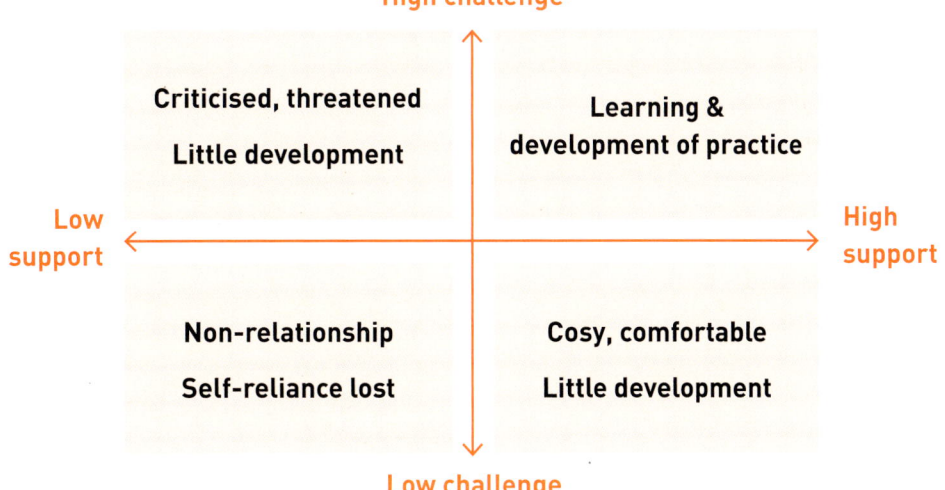

It is clear from this that, if a foster carer is to learn and develop, they require a supervisory relationship that mixes high levels of support with high levels of challenge when needed. In order to do this, the supervising social worker needs to create an open and honest working relationship with the foster carer.

If a balanced mix of support and challenge is not created, the foster carer will be deprived of the opportunity to develop their skills and abilities. If the supervising social worker only provides minimal support, with infrequent visits or contact, or the carer does not feel heard and appreciated by their worker, the working relationship will not be positive. The carer will not have confidence in their worker or feel able to learn from them.

On the other hand, when a supervising social worker provides a foster carer with a high level of support, with frequent visits, and establishes a close relationship with them, their familiarity with the carer can make it harder for them to provide constructive challenge. Therefore, a supervising social worker should always be cautious that their relationship with a foster carer does not slip from being a professional one to that of friendship. As Cleaver and Rose explain (2020, p 90):

> ...where carers are well known to professionals, this can lead to a loss of objectivity. A supervising social worker's sense of loyalty to "their carers" may threaten impartiality, result in over-optimism and undermine the ability to safeguard children.

However, if the foster carer believes that they are being challenged regularly, they may feel criticised, and this may block their ability to learn and develop. Therefore, the supervising social worker needs to perform a careful balancing act in order to maintain the right mix of high support and high challenge.

PRIORITISING AND PREPARING FOR SUPERVISION

It is important to ensure that both parties view supervision as an essential appointment that can only be delayed in an emergency. If a supervising social worker frequently cancels sessions or arrives late, it sends the message to the foster carer that supervision is not a priority in their working day, undermining its significance. Similarly, if a foster carer frequently rearranges supervision, the supervising social worker may assume that the carer is disengaging and does not see themselves as a vital member of the network of professionals working with the child.

One supervising social worker gave an example of a foster carer who was always welcoming but tended to take phone calls during supervision or cut sessions short because they had to get to another appointment.

The worker explained that, as a result, she did not feel the carer was in a position to benefit from these sessions. She resolved this by amending the existing supervision agreement to include details such as what each party would do to prepare for the session (including clearly marking the time of the session in diaries), as well as agreements to arrive on time and not to take non-emergency calls during the session. The amendments were designed to represent the commitment of both parties, rather than criticising the foster carer in any way.

Many fostering services use a supervision agreement from the point of approval of a foster carer, as it provides clear details of the service's expectations of, and their commitment to, the carer. The service should negotiate the terms of this agreement with the foster carer, and it should cover:

- how often the supervision sessions will take place;
- who will be present (one or both carers? Other adults in the household? The carer's children?);
- the arrangements for supervising the secondary carer if they will not be present at the sessions;
- where the supervision will take place;
- the approximate length of each session;
- the key aspects for discussion (the emotional health and well-being of those in the household, Training, Support and Development standards, training, the foster carer's development, the current care needs and care plans for children in placement, payments, communication with services, etc);
- that any concerns or complaints about the foster carer will be discussed;
- the circumstances under which supervision can be postponed;
- the timescales for rescheduling postponed sessions;
- how supervision will be recorded and when the carer will receive a copy of the supervision record;
- the process for raising issues about the accuracy of the supervision record.

According to a Practice Tool created by Research in Practice, the Tavistock and Portman NHS Foundation Trust, the University of Sussex and Goldsmiths, University of London, 'the supervisory relationship is one of inherent power dynamics at play' (2020, p 7). This should be borne in mind when constructing a supervision contract with a foster carer. The fostering service will have procedures in place, regulations to follow, and expectations of the carer. The supervising social worker will represent their service in this relationship, as well as being in a personal position of power over the carer because of the knowledge they hold. In order to acknowledge this, but also to create a mutual working relationship, the contract should also reflect the carer's expectations of the worker.

An additional factor to consider is that it is the norm for supervision sessions to be held in a foster carer's own home rather than in a formal setting. This can mean that there is a relaxed atmosphere, which could lead to a lack of challenge. Similarly, because discussions are happening in the carer's domain where they have control, it could lead to a reluctance to challenge on behalf of the supervising social worker.

Preparation for a supervision session is important. The supervising social worker should make sure that they have:

- read the previous supervision records;
- reviewed the carer's chronology and noted any significant patterns;
- read any diary recordings submitted by the carer since the last supervision;
- studied any regular recordings about the child in placement by the child's social worker (if these are accessible to the supervising social worker) to identify areas for discussion;
- checked the carer's current training record and Personal Development Plan, and identified any needs;
- ensured that all statutory checks, such as DBS checks, on the fostering household are up to date.

RECORD-KEEPING PRACTICES

Fostering services may have varying processes for recording supervision, but it is vital that a recording is made and produced in a timely manner, and that a copy of the supervision record is available to the foster carer. When concerns are raised with carers about their practice, and this leads to a presentation to a fostering panel to consider their suitability to foster, it is not unusual for a supervising social worker to state that they discussed a particular issue with the foster carer in supervision, and for the carer to state that the matter was not discussed and that they did not receive a supervision record of the discussion. Sometimes this impasse can be avoided by sending copies of supervision records to the carer electronically with "read receipt" requests and asking them to raise any concerns within 14 days of receiving the records. These actions can all be recorded in the carer's file.

On a more positive note, sending records of the discussion to foster carers enables them to read these at their leisure, reflect on them, and refer back to discussions in the future if a particular issue arises again.

IDENTIFYING AND ADAPTING TO FOSTER CARERS' LEARNING STYLES

In the early stages of developing the supervision relationship, the supervising social worker should try to ascertain the foster carer's learning style, as this can help them to shape future sessions. Experts often refer to seven main types of learning style, based on the work of researchers such as Fleming and Mills (1992), and Gardner (1983): visual, aural, verbal, physical, logical, social, and solitary.

Honey and Mumford (1986) described the following four learning styles:

Learning style	Type of learner	Learning preference
Activists	Hands on	Trial and error
Reflectors	Tell me	Briefed before proceeding
Theorists	Convince me	Clarity – does this make sense?
Pragmatists	Show me	Likes an expert to demonstrate

Being aware of a foster carer's preferred learning style will help the supervising social worker to convey information to them effectively. It may also help them to structure the supervision sessions in the most appropriate way. The worker should also reflect on their own learning style, consider whether it complements or conflicts with the foster carer's style, and explore how they can address any issues that arise from this. It is worth noting, however, that while some fostering services leave supervision session structure to the social worker's discretion, others have specific structures that they prefer their workers to use.

When developing the supervisory relationship, it is important to establish a structure for the supervision sessions that works for both the supervising social worker and the foster carer. Some carers, for example, may prefer to raise ongoing issues about children in placement before focusing on their own issues or development needs, while others may prefer to address their development needs first and then take time to think through issues relating to their current foster children. The supervising social worker may also have a format that they normally use for supervision, and some negotiation may be needed in order to ensure that the process works for both parties.

SUPERVISION MODELS

1. The 4x4x4 model

Morrison (2005), and later with Wonnacott (2010), presented a 4x4x4 model of supervision. As part of this, they mentioned four key elements, which are detailed below alongside the stages of a supervisory session that could be held with a foster carer.

	What this means in the supervision of foster carers
Experience	Considering what has happened to date, both in relation to the child's placement generally and any specific incidents.
Reflection	Investigating what the carer is thinking and feeling, as well as what the child in placement may be feeling.
Analysis	Encouraging the carer to use their knowledge and experience when looking at the situation from all perspectives.
Action planning	Establishing what the carer wants to achieve, agreeing the steps that they are going to take to reach their goals, and establishing whether they need to seek assistance from other parties.

2. Social pedagogy in foster care

A similar model of supervision to Morrison's was proposed by the Fostering Network at their conference, 'Head, heart and hands: introducing social pedagogy into foster care', in 2015.

Social pedagogy is based on the concept of working together to learn and develop throughout life and using reflection as part of this learning. It concentrates on developing the whole person and giving them learning opportunities. In order to help foster carers develop to their potential, the Fostering Network adopted a model known as 'the Four Fs', an approach devised by Greenaway (1992) in his Active Reviewing Cycle. The Fostering Network incorporated this into their training materials and suggested that fostering services use this model for carer supervision.

Figure 2: The Four Fs

Facts	Feelings
An objective description of what has happened	A description of the feelings connected to the facts

Findings	Future
What sense can we make of the facts and feelings? What can we learn from looking at both?	What can we put into action? What can we do better or differently next time?

(Fostering Network, 2016b)

The Fostering Network described this as being a "very simple" approach, but one that would assist foster carers in separating facts from feelings.

3. Strengths-based supervision

Tim Odell, writing in 2008, discussed the use of a strengths-based approach when supporting foster carers, and this has been developing over time. It concentrates on recognising and developing the individual carer's self-determination and strengths. The supervising social worker should encourage the carer to identify, value and understand their strengths and abilities. Carers are encouraged to set their own goals, learn about the resources available to them, and focus on positivity and hope.

To enable this approach, the supervising social worker needs to view the carer as a partner and work with them in a collaborative way to plan for and support the child or young person being cared for. When a worker enables a carer to adopt this approach to fostering, they are also role-modelling an approach that the foster carer can use with the child in their care.

4. The Signs of Safety model

This strengths-based model was originally created in Australia for use in child protection (Department of Child Protection, 2011) but it is now used by many UK local authorities. Part of its original appeal was the fact that it involved parents as partners in child protection conferences. This concept of partnership working translates well to foster care as it is crucial for the supervising social worker to create professional partnerships with foster carers.

The key questions asked during safeguarding conferences when this approach is used can easily be applied to fostering:

- What is working well?
- What are we worried about?
- What needs to happen?

The directness of the questions asked, and the solution-focused nature of this model, means that many foster carers find this approach easy to understand and to fully engage in.

5. The Secure Base model

Whilst not a supervision model itself, this model can be adapted for supervision purposes. This is a framework for caregiving devised by Schofield and Beek (2014), and based on attachment theory, as well as knowledge of child development and family relationships. It promotes the development of resilience by advocating the provision of security, the development of self-esteem, and the capacity for reflection.

Figure 3: The Secure Base model

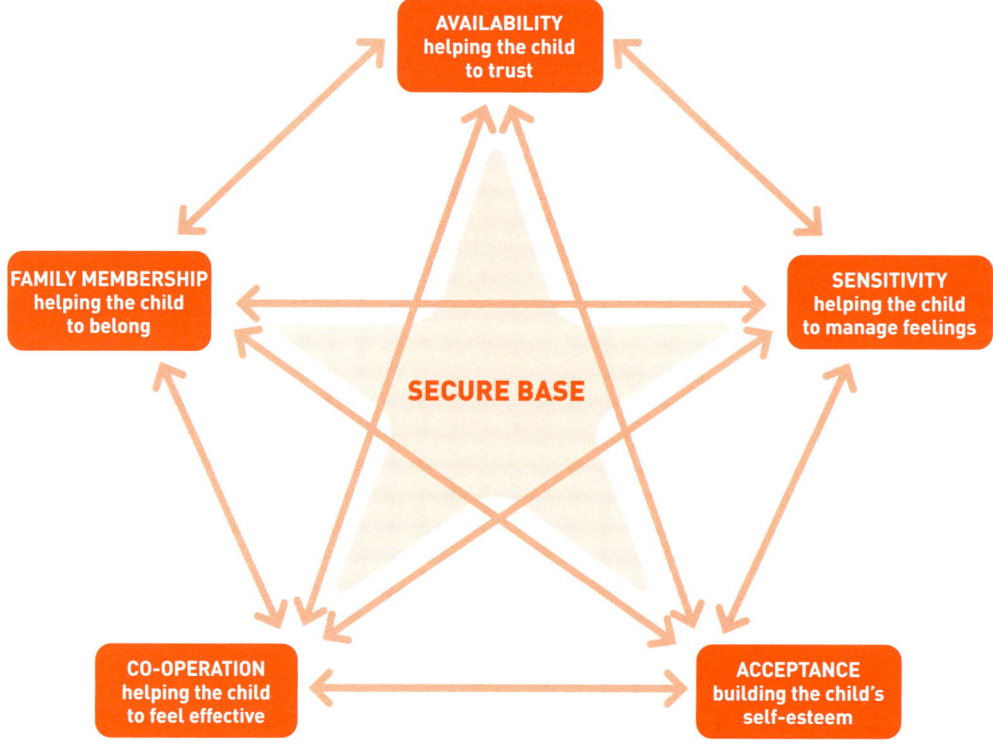

(Schofield and Beek, 2014)

This model can be used with foster carers in regular supervision sessions in order to consider how the child is developing relationships within their household, and what changes have been seen in the child's ability to manage their behaviour and express their feelings. Foster carers can be asked, for example, to identify when the child is beginning to trust them or other members of the fostering household, and consider further ways in which trust could be built. By progressing around the points of the star, discussing the various aspects of the approach for a child, small positive signs of attachment and new creative ways of building on these can often be identified.

It may also be useful in cases where the placement appears to be "stuck" and to require a fresh approach in order to allow the child to continue to flourish in the foster home.

ADDITIONAL ISSUES TO CONSIDER

Supervising family and friends carers

Special consideration also needs to be given to supervision of family and friends carers (also known as kinship carers). These are carers whom local authorities have approved to care for related children, such as their grandchildren, nieces and nephews, etc. They will, ideally, have been approved within the 16-week timeframe required by regulation 24 of the Care Planning, Placement and Case Review (England) Regulations 2010. Therefore, they may not have had access to an introductory fostering course or had time to absorb the professionals' requirements of foster carers, as their focus will have been on changing their family lives in order to accommodate the new additions to their homes, often at short notice, and attending meetings and court proceedings. The concept of supervision may be quite alien to them and the supervising social worker will need to explain the requirements that mainstream carers become familiar with through their preparatory training courses and from their pre-approval research and reading.

In recent discussions with the author, supervising social workers suggested that, in these cases, there needs to be a gradual introduction to formally structured supervision that initially allows free discussion. Structure should then be added over time as the carer undertakes training, attends meetings, and gains a greater understanding of their role and the requirements of being a foster carer.

In situations where carers are new to fostering and have not yet fully developed their skillsets, it is important for the supervising social worker to encourage their development by helping them to explore possible solutions to dilemmas without being directive. The worker may well have a solution to an issue in mind, but a carer's development will be enhanced if they are able to explore the options available and find a solution themselves.

"Set up to fail syndrome" and ways to resolve this

This concept was described by Manzine and Barsoux (2002), who believed that the actions of a manager could impact on an employee's performance. The concept can be transferred to the supervisory relationship between a supervising social worker and a foster carer.

If a supervising social worker is critical of, or too directive with, a foster carer, the carer may experience what is known as "set up to fail syndrome". The diagram below shows how this can occur.

Figure 4: Set up to fail syndrome

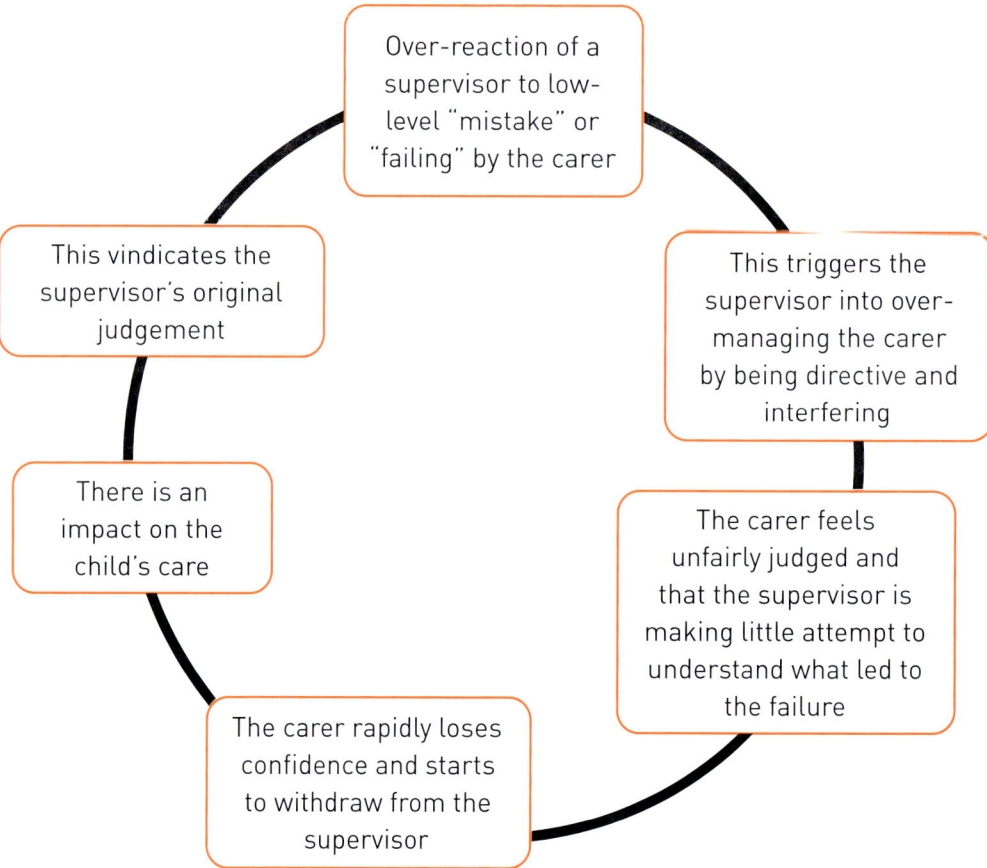

For example, a new foster carer may try to set boundaries for a fostered child using the concept of "time out", which they feel worked well with their own children. However, the supervising social worker may tell the carer that they should not use this approach, explaining that "time out" excludes and isolates the child, and that social work favours alternative approaches, such as "time in", where the child sits quietly with the carer for a few minutes. While the advice from the supervising social worker is sound, the carer may feel that their parenting skills are being questioned. They may then begin to doubt their skills and be reluctant to set boundaries for the child. This will impact on the care that the child receives and could negatively affect their sense of security. The supervising social worker may then observe a child who is not having boundaries set for them, and conclude that the foster carer does not have the skills to do this.

The worker could use a coaching method with the carer instead. Coaching is a structured, developmental approach, which can be used to handle a specific issue, and which focuses on achieving specific, immediate goals. There are various coaching methods available, for example, the GROW model (originally created in the 1980s and updated in Passmore, 2010).

GROW stands for:
- **G**oal
- **R**eality
- **O**ptions
- **W**ill or **W**rap Up

The basics of the model are as follows.

Figure 5: The GROW model

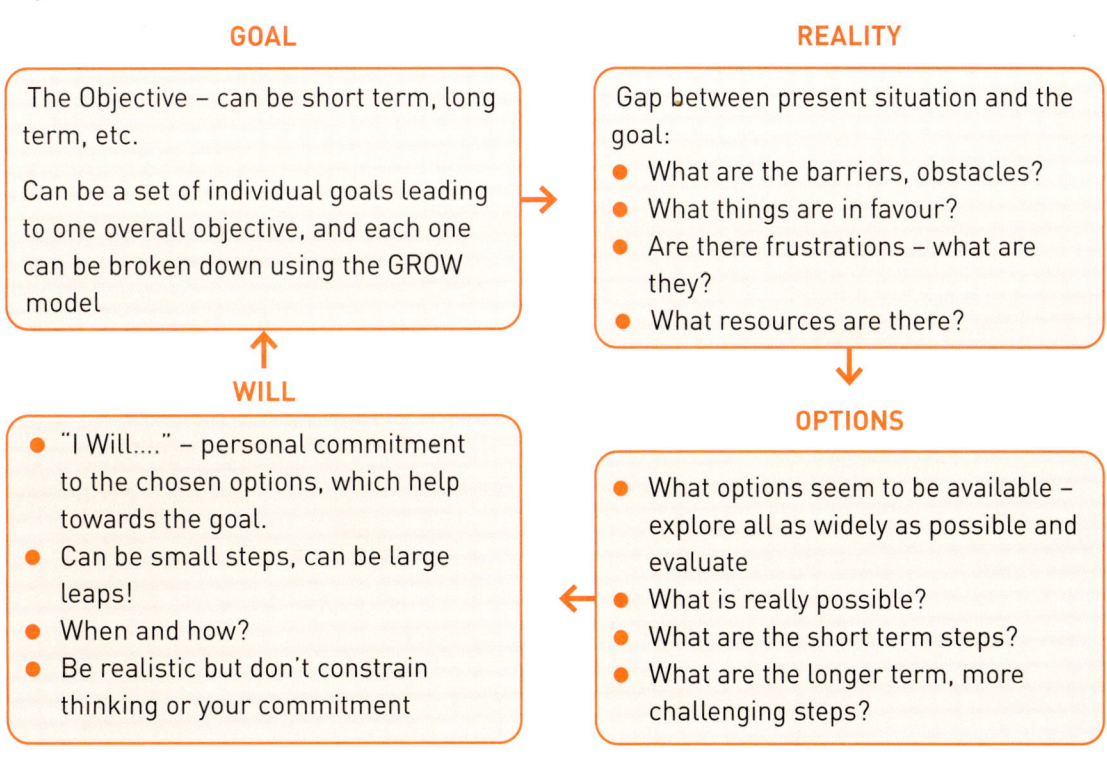

(Coates, 2013)

When using this model, the supervising social worker should encourage the foster carer to:

- state the issue they wish to resolve;
- think through all of the possible options and responses;
- choose an option;
- break this option down into manageable steps;
- be clear about how and when these steps will occur.

If we take this approach when dealing with the issue of "time out" or "time in" (discussed above), the worker could start a conversation with the carer about the fact that boundary setting seems to be an issue with the child placed, and that perhaps the worker and carer could look at the causes of this in more detail, as well as identifying the desired outcomes, rather than appearing to be critical of the carer's chosen actions.

- In the Goal phase, the worker would ask the carer what they want to achieve and help them to identify goals. These could be, for example, that the child listens to requests, responds to them, does not engage in risky behaviour, understands negotiation, or finds new behaviour strategies.

- In the Reality phase, the worker would ask the carer open-ended questions to explore the details of the situation, the strategies that have been tried, how these have worked, the resources that are available, and who has been affected by the issue.

- In the Options phase, the worker would encourage the carer to consider all possible responses by asking them questions such as:
  - If they could start again, what would they do?
  - What would they advise someone in a similar situation to do?
  - What would move things forward?

- In the Will, or Wrap Up, section, the worker would encourage the carer to select one of the options, identify any obstacles, work out how to overcome these, and break the task down into achievable steps. In the example above, this could mean deciding not to use "time in" or "time out", but instead to intervene at a much earlier stage so as to divert the child before a situation escalates, or to role model appropriate behaviour as a family.

This model of coaching is adaptable. While it can be used within formal supervision sessions, it can also be used during informal discussions when a relevant issue emerges, or during phone calls between the worker and carer when there is a problem to be resolved.

SUMMARY

The issues discussed in this chapter highlight the complexity of the role of the supervising social worker, who needs to fulfil their fostering service's requirements for the development and support of carers, while creating a working relationship that is supportive, but that also involves challenging carers where appropriate. An additional tension can be generated by the fact that supervision is offered within the foster carer's own home. The worker is operating on the carer's home territory, and is present at their invitation. This can be problematic, because the informality of the situation can result in the relaxation of boundaries or make it more challenging for the worker to convey difficult messages.

The chapters that follow examine the process of supervision in practice in more depth, highlighting the supervising social worker's role as they support their foster carers. We first consider how the worker can support new foster carers to understand the responsibilities, demands and challenges that they will face.

Chapter 5
Supporting foster carers to understand their role

This chapter focuses on foster carers' induction to fostering, looks at how the working relationship between supervising social worker and foster carer is developed, and also considers how other support mechanisms can be established for the foster carer and their family members.

Once a carer has been approved by a fostering service, their fostering experience begins. It is the service's responsibility to ensure that the carer receives a comprehensive introduction to the legal requirements of fostering and to the service's own policies and procedures. The supervising social worker will play a key role in this, and some of the main tasks that they are responsible for performing during this initial fostering period are described below.

PROVIDING INDUCTIONS

Section 20.1 of the Fostering Service National Minimum Standards (2011) states that all new foster carers must receive an induction. The exact content of this varies from service to service, but can include the points below:

- an introduction to their supervising social worker, if this is not their assessing social worker;
- an introduction to the service's key staff members;
- the provision of the service's fostering handbook and an opportunity to discuss its content;
- the provision of a Foster Care Agreement, which must be signed by all parties;
- the development of a safer care policy for the household;
- the provision of an identity badge;
- linking the foster carer with a mentor;

- the provision of the service's training brochure and the development of an individual training plan;

- introductions to peer support groups and fostering associations;

- an explanation of the process for expenses claims;

- the provision of the Training, Support and Development standards workbook, if this has not been provided during the assessment stage;

- ensuring that the foster carer has a lockable storage facility for confidential documentation;

- ensuring that the foster carer is familiar with the correct process for recording and submitting recordings about the child or young person placed with them;

- ensuring that the foster carer understands the need to record and report safeguarding concerns (this is discussed further in Chapter 10);

- the provision of information about statutory processes relating to foster homes;

- the opportunity for the foster carer to shadow experienced foster carers.

> **GOOD PRACTICE EXAMPLE**
>
> In one independent fostering service, which has a team of parent and child foster carers, carers are not able to take a first placement until they have shadowed an experienced foster carer and provided three days of respite foster care.
>
> (Pathway Care, Ashburton, Devon)

In some services, the assessing social worker becomes the foster carer's supervising social worker after the fostering panel has taken place. This can be advantageous because they know the foster carer well, have established a working relationship with them, and are aware of the family's unique characteristics. They are, therefore, well placed to discuss a possible match with a child, based on their detailed knowledge of the fostering family.

In other services, the foster carer transfers from an assessing social worker to a supervising social worker immediately after approval. In such cases, the carer needs to be introduced to their supervising social worker as soon as possible after the fostering decision-maker has approved them. Some services make plans for the supervising social worker to be present at the approval panel meeting or to meet the foster carer when it has concluded. This means that the foster carer knows which social worker will be supporting them from the outset. However, this could be seen as pre-empting the outcome of the decision-maker's deliberations. The fostering panel only makes a recommendation to the decision-maker, and the final decision on the carer's approval needs to be made within seven working days of the decision-maker receiving the recommendation and final set of panel minutes. While it is rare for a decision-maker to disagree with a panel's recommendation, it can happen. Therefore, introducing a supervising social worker prior to this point may raise the prospective carer's expectations that approval will be granted, potentially leading to additional disappointment and confusion for them if they are not approved.

Given that foster carers form working relationships with their assessing social workers, this partnership needs to be transferred to the supervising social worker (if this will involve a different worker). If possible, the supervising social worker's first visit to the foster carer should be carried out with the assessing social worker also present. The foster carer's strengths and vulnerabilities, as identified by the assessing social worker, should be discussed during this meeting, so that the supervising social worker can continue to support the carer in these areas.

The supervising social worker should read the foster carer's assessment report and the minutes from the fostering panel prior to their initial visit, so that they are aware of any issues raised by the panel and any actions required, for example, the worker may need to source a specific training course for the carer. During the initial visit, the supervising social worker should clarify whether the carer has received full details of the fostering service's policies and procedures. They should also ensure that the carer has all the service's contact details, so that they can get in touch with someone both within and outside of standard office hours.

It may be relevant, at this point, for the supervising social worker to ask the carer whether they are happy to accept direct requests for placements from the fostering service and the emergency duty system. If they are not confident enough for this, the worker can filter any requests for initial placements until all parties are certain that the carer feels able to respond to these directly. Even when a foster carer is happy to take direct requests from the duty service, they should be encouraged to discuss the child's needs with their supervising social worker before offering to care for that child. There have been situations where carers returning to panel for their first annual review have stated that they accepted the first placement offered because they were excited about the prospect, but that, with the benefit of hindsight, it was not appropriate for them. Carers in this position can feel deskilled and begin to wonder whether fostering is the right option for them. The first year of fostering is a time to build a carer's confidence. Therefore, initially, it may be appropriate for the supervising social worker to consider placements on their behalf. The worker could also assist the carer by helping them to draw up a checklist of questions to refer to when contacted by a duty worker about the possible placement of a child. This will enable the carer to acquire as much relevant information about the child and their particular needs as possible.

In many agencies, it is standard practice for all placements to be discussed with the foster carer's supervising social worker or their manager during the carer's first year after approval, in order to aid the matching process.

CREATING WORKING RELATIONSHIPS WITH FOSTER CARERS

During the first few months after a foster carer's approval, the supervising social worker's role is to make sure that the carer feels supported and able to seek advice and guidance, whilst also ensuring that they understand and are complying with fostering regulations and standards. Therefore, the two parties need to build a working relationship that enables the carer to share their thoughts and feelings, and allows the worker to maintain professional boundaries at all times. This means that the worker must perform a delicate balancing act, creating a close and trust-based relationship with the carer, whilst establishing enough authority to enable them to raise compliance or practice concerns when required. As the research review by Cosis Brown *et al* (2014) has shown (see Chapter 3), foster carers sometimes refer to their supervising social worker as their support worker, something which is, in part, correct. However, supervising social workers need to avoid slipping into the role of a foster carer's friend, particularly when they have worked with them for a long time.

In discussion with the author, a group of supervising social workers highlighted the issue of balancing professional and personal relationships with foster carers as one of the most difficult areas to negotiate. Foster carers and social workers are part of a professional network. Social workers often share personal information with their fellow professionals (for example, team members) when working with them over time, and many find that sharing a little detail can build a trusting working relationship of equals. They may, therefore, be tempted to share information with foster carers, particularly as they know full details of the carer's life history. However, sharing too much personal information with a carer can make it difficult to challenge their professional practice if this becomes necessary.

It may be appropriate for the supervising social worker to share some non-identifying information about their family situation with foster carers. For example, they could say that they are a parent and therefore can empathise with a situation, without providing any details about their children and their personal histories. It may also be appropriate for the worker to share their personal feelings at times, so that the carer is aware that the worker identifies with their situation. However, this needs to be contained and within boundaries.

The group of supervising social workers mentioned above also discussed the dilemma that they faced in respect of how accessible they should be to carers. Foster carers are provided with their supervising social worker's work phone number, but should their calls be answered 24 hours a day, seven days a week, or should carers be directed to an emergency duty responder out of office hours? The supervising social workers felt that they often made themselves available to foster carers because they knew their situation and might be able to resolve an issue quickly, while the emergency duty system might not have the key information to hand. However, this can lead to dependency and expectations on behalf of foster carers that cannot always be met.

Each fostering service will have its own policy on this issue (and some will have their own out-of-hours support for foster carers), but the individual supervising social worker may have to gauge their response based on their knowledge of the carer and their current situation. It may be appropriate to ask carers to only phone their own supervising social worker before a certain time each day, and to contact the emergency duty system at other times, or to only ring the supervising social worker outside of normal working hours in emergencies.

Working relationships with two foster carers

When two foster carers are involved in a placement, the supervising social worker should also think about the roles played by each carer when beginning to build a relationship with them. If only the primary foster carer will be attending supervision sessions regularly, how will the worker build and sustain a relationship with the secondary carer? It is essential to build relationships with both carers in order to have an open and honest dialogue, and so that the worker can gauge the impact of fostering on all parties accurately. The worker could begin to establish rapport with the secondary carer by:

- booking supervision sessions at a time when the secondary carer is likely to be at home;
- phoning the secondary carer to check whether they have any concerns about fostering;
- making additional visits to the home when both carers are likely to be present;
- encouraging both carers to attend support groups and training sessions;
- arranging to meet with the secondary carer at a minimum of every three months, in line with good practice recommendations.

When a working relationship does not work out

There are times when the relationship between a supervising social worker and a carer does not work. This may be due to their personalities, or to differing approaches to communication. If difficulties occur, the supervising social worker should discuss this with their manager at an early stage to ensure that a positive working relationship with the carer can be maintained by the service. Prior to any change of supervising social worker, the issues causing strain should be explored and attempts at resolution should be made. Consideration should also be given as to whether the carer could be describing a poor working relationship as a diversion technique in order to avoid the service focusing on the quality of fostering being provided, as was found in some of the case reviews explored in Chapter 3.

When a change of supervising social worker is necessary, it should not be viewed as a failure on the part of the worker or an indicator that the carer is difficult to work with. Instead, it should simply be seen as a poor initial match. However, some services consider that, as professionals, foster carers and supervising social workers should always be able to work together. Whilst this is a valid argument, there is also a need to acknowledge that tensions in a working relationship can inhibit people from working to their full capacity, and this can impact on the child in placement, who should receive the best possible standards of care from the fostering service.

PROVIDING KEY INFORMATION TO FOSTER CARERS

During a foster carer's induction, it is important that the supervising social worker restates the information about the regulations for foster homes and the individual service's requirements for carers that should have been provided during the carer's initial training and assessment. This includes the areas listed below.

Explaining and conducting unannounced visits

NMS 10.5 requires that 'the foster home is inspected annually, without appointment, by the fostering service to make sure that it continues to meet the needs of the foster children' (DfE, 2011, p 22), while NMS 21.8 states that all foster carers should receive 'at least one unannounced visit a year' (p 43).

These visits are usually carried out by the supervising social worker, although some services may use other workers within their team in order to introduce an element of independence. The supervising social worker should explain to the foster carer during their induction that these visits will take place, and should make it clear that this is a requirement of the carer's registration. This will help to minimise the chances of any issues arising when the visits are carried out. The supervising social worker should also ensure that the carer understands the purpose of unannounced visits, which is to observe the standards of care being provided to the child. This includes checking that household standards are consistent throughout the home, and that the accommodation provided to any fostered child staying there is of a similar standard to that provided to everyone else in the property. Whenever possible on an unannounced visit, the child should be seen by the worker and their views sought.

During the visits, the supervising social worker should look at all areas of the property, including the garden and any outbuildings, to ensure that there are no safety issues that could place a child at risk. Some services combine these unannounced visits with updated health and safety property assessments.

Where staffing levels allow, it can be beneficial to carry out more than one unannounced visit a year. This will enable the worker to view the property during different seasons, and may allow them to see family life within the fostering household from different perspectives. Further insight can be obtained by varying the time of visits, for example, visiting at breakfast time or during early evening, so that the foster child can be seen when they are immersed in family life. The worker should make it clear to the carer that they cannot refuse these visits except in exceptional circumstances, such as when a member of the household is seriously ill and cannot be disturbed.

All unannounced visits should be recorded. The example form in Appendix 1, provided by Lighthouse Fostering (an independent fostering service based in Kent), shows the issues that should be covered and included in the report. In this example, the service focuses on the child's lived experience in the household and the observed interactions in the foster home, as well as on conditions within the home.

Health and safety assessments

A foster carer's assessing social worker will carry out a home safety check as part of the assessment process. However, during the induction, the supervising social worker should make it clear to the carer that they, in partnership with the worker, have an obligation to constantly review their home in order to identify and resolve safety issues. The supervising social worker should discuss the fact that the carer should balance the need to keep children safe with the need to ensure that they can have a normal family life. They should also make sure that the carer has informed the companies providing their home and car insurance that they are now fostering, as failing to do so may invalidate their policies and not all health and safety assessments cover this.

Health and safety checks are required to ensure that the following NMS are met:

> *10.1 The foster home can comfortably accommodate all who live there including where appropriate any suitable aids and adaptations provided and fitted by suitably trained staff when caring for a disabled child.*
>
> *10.2 The foster home is warm, adequately furnished and decorated, is maintained to a good standard of cleanliness and hygiene and is in good order throughout. Outdoor spaces which are part of the premises are safe, secure and well maintained.*
>
> *10.3 Foster carers are trained in health and safety issues and have guidelines on their health and safety responsibilities. Avoidable hazards are removed as is consistent with a family home.*
>
> (DfE, 2011, p 22)

Supervising social workers also need to stress to foster carers that these checks are a requirement of fostering regulations and that there is an onus on them to report any relevant changes in their home conditions. Some supervising social workers review health and safety as part of their unannounced visits, while others do this prior to annual reviews, but these reviews should always be on their agenda.

The supervising social worker should ensure that the foster carer is aware that they need to notify them if:

- there are new people planning to live in the foster home;
- adults in the household change their employment, especially when their new role is home-based and clients or colleagues may visit the home, or the person is working shifts;
- a new pet is added to the household, as a pet assessment may need to take place;
- there are building works in progress at the home or major changes are being made to the outside area, such the installation of a pond or hot tub, as these need to be inspected to ensure that all safety requirements are met;
- guns are being stored in the household, as these must be stored in a lockable gun cabinet and only the gun licence/key holder should know where the key is kept. The worker should also ensure that the ammunition is being stored separately from the firearms – ideally, it should be kept in another building.

The supervising social worker should ensure that the health and safety assessment is updated to take account of any new risks identified whenever there is a new placement. If there is a proposal that fostered children over the age of three should share a bedroom, the worker should conduct a separate bedroom sharing risk assessment. It is also good practice to conduct a health and safety assessment each year as a minimum requirement, even if no new placements have been made.

Each fostering service tends to produce its own health and safety checklist. However, a good example of a health and safety assessment form (along with excellent advice) is included in Adams' book, *Undertaking Checks and References in Fostering and Adoption Assessments* (2019a, pp 141–144).

Medical checks

Every foster carer should have a medical assessment as part of their fostering assessment, but services have differing requirements in terms of when and how these should be updated. Good practice is to carry out an update of the foster carer's health every two or three years, or if a substantial change in a carer's health has been observed. CoramBAAF has created a report template that can be used to undertake this. However, some services prefer to use their own format, while others ask their carers to complete a self-assessment form that may be reviewed by the service's medical adviser.

The supervising social worker should ensure that these medical assessments are completed in line with service policy, but also highlight the need for an early assessment if they become aware of a health condition that may be impacting on a foster carer's ability to meet a child's needs. It is important for the worker to help carers to understand that fostering is a demanding occupation and that they need to ensure that all of their own health needs are met in order to provide care for a child. The worker should also stress that, in many cases, having a medical condition will not mean that the carer will need to stop fostering; however, it may mean that the carer will need to be reassessed and they may require some personal support so that they can continue to fulfil their role.

This may be particularly relevant for family and friends carers, many of whom are grandparents and likely to be older, and therefore to have more underlying health conditions, than non-connected foster carers. As a result, they may worry that if they experience changes to their health, it will mean that they can no longer care for the child. The worker should ensure that the carer understands that the child's needs come first and that, whenever possible, if the child's primary need is to be with that particular carer, additional support should be provided to enable that placement to continue.

Disclosure and Barring Service checks

These are checks used to record and analyse a person's past (in Scotland, they are undertaken by the Vetting and Barring Service). They look specifically at any convictions, cautions, reprimands and warnings they may have received. They are carried out at the point of assessment for foster carers, and most services review them at least every three years.

The supervising social worker's role is to explain to each carer that these checks will be repeated regularly and that if they or members of the fostering household commit any kind of offence, they should share this information with the worker immediately, so that the service can make any relevant checks, complete any reports required by the service, and consider the implications for any child in the foster home. The safer caring policy (below) may need to be updated, for example, as there might be a risk to the child in placement.

National Minimum Standards

Both fostering services and fostering panels consider whether foster carers meet the National Minimum Standards (NMS). As mentioned in Chapter 2, in England the NMS are issued under section 23 of the Care Standards Act, and were last updated in 2011. They cover the values and principles expected of foster care providers, and services are expected to ensure that they meet and exceed these standards. The NMS are based on the concept that all children should have enjoyable childhoods and be able to benefit from excellent parenting and education.

The role of the supervising social worker in relation to the NMS is to:

- ensure that they are conversant with them;
- ensure that the carers they are supporting are familiar with them; and
- assess whether the carers are providing care that would enable the service to meet these standards.

Where a supervising social worker organises a support group for their foster carers, they could usefully hold discussions about the NMS and encourage the group to share ideas about how the service can meet and exceed particular standards. This will help to reinforce the concept of continuous improvement and development of foster carers to provide the best possible experience for children in care.

Whether they are working with foster carers as individual households or as a group, the supervising social worker could identify one of the key NMS and ask the foster carer/s to think about what that standard would look like in practice when caring for a child. For example, NMS 3.2 requires foster carers to 'provide an environment and culture that promotes, models and supports positive behaviour' (DfE, 2011, p 12).

The supervising social worker could ask each carer to describe how they would translate this into practice and what these actions would look like in everyday life in their household. This type of discussion could also be undertaken with carers to enable them to complete their Training, Support and Development (TSD) standards.

Safer caring policies

It is good practice for fostering services to have a safer caring policy in place for each fostering household, and an individual safer caring policy in place for each child in foster care. Slade (2012) states that 'family safer caring plans are documents that are a means of making sure that everyone in the fostering household understands the principles and rules for living together' (p 79). The fostering household's safer caring policy should be reviewed as part of the preparation for the carer's annual review, and should be updated when there are any significant household changes. The worker should ensure that all members of the household are familiar with the safer caring policy.

The individual child's safer caring policy should be created at the point of placement and reviewed when a new placement is made, whenever there are any significant safeguarding issues, or when changes for the child take place.

These safer caring policies are designed to ensure the well-being and safety of both the child and the fostering household, and to protect them, as far as possible, from abuse or allegations of abuse. As part of the safer caring policy, individual risk assessments may be needed relating to the specific child. These may relate to risks *for* the child or young person, such as absconding, self-harming or use of drugs and alcohol, risks *to* the young person from family members or associates, and risks *from* one young person towards another. There may also be specific risks to the foster family, for example, from a young person's associates. Any risk assessment should clearly detail the risk, the indicators that an issue might be occurring, and the plan to mitigate that risk, which should be agreed by all relevant parties.

CoramBAAF has created a Form R for risk assessment, which can be used alongside Adams' guide, *Devising and Updating Risk Assessment and Management Plans in Fostering* (2021).

Record-keeping

The supervising social worker should explain to foster carers that they will monitor and quality assure the records that the carers keep in respect of placements during the first year that they are fostering, and that they will continue to quality assure recordings throughout their fostering career. This includes ensuring that the carers clearly differentiate between their observations and their opinions when creating them. This is a skill that foster carers develop over time, and a subject that the supervising social worker can discuss with them on an ongoing basis during supervision. A guiding principle is for the carer to keep in mind that the child is the key audience, as the records, of course, are about them, and they may well read these in the near or distant future (some carers encourage young people to contribute to their diary recordings). That does not mean that negative or difficult content should be avoided; more that it should be written in such a way that allows for understanding and does not shame the child. Children can also be greatly helped by looking back at the progress they have made. Many services are now writing any reports about a young person directly to the child, and this would be a good skill for carers to develop.

Some services provide their foster carers with a template for record-keeping, while others prefer to allow them to use their own personal formats. Whichever format carers use, the information that they record needs to be evidenced and non-judgemental. Supervising social workers need to ensure that their carers are informed about the availability of training courses on recording skills, and should facilitate their attendance on these.

When working with some foster carers, the supervising social worker will need to discuss specific issues, such as the quantity of record keeping required, the need to achieve a balance between positives and areas of concern, and the timelines for the submission of written records. They can also assist the carer by providing an example of a comprehensive record (of an imaginary child) at the start of their fostering career, and constructive criticism of the records that the carer submits to them. Good record keeping is not only important as a record of the child's time with the carer, but can help to protect the carer against allegations.

Storage of children's records and documentation should be discussed with the foster carer before their first placement. Some services allow carers to access their dedicated IT systems and store all documentation and recordings there. Others provide carers with encrypted USB sticks that must be kept in a locked drawer and returned at the end of the child's placement. Other services ask carers to store recordings on their own home computers and to email these to the service, in which case carers' computers need to be password protected. Copies of all documentation held by the carer should be placed on the child's electronic file when the placement ends, and all records need to be deleted permanently from the carer's computer once the child has left the placement. If paper copies of any documentation have been held, these should be returned to the fostering service to either be placed on the child's file or destroyed.

In the past, foster carers were often advised by trainers and social workers to keep duplicate records relating to children placed with them in case a historical allegation of abuse was made against them. However, supervising social workers should be very clear that this should not occur, as there are no legal grounds for a carer to retain such records. More information on this issue, as well as other matters relating to data protection, can be found in the guide by Adams and Jordan (2019).

The supervising social worker should also, at an early stage, discuss the importance of constructing physical or virtual memory boxes with the foster carer. Memory boxes provide children with a record of their stay in a foster household, and catalogue events that have occurred and the child's achievements while living there. The memory box should be provided to the child in its entirety when they leave the placement, but should also be available for them to view during their stay in the household.

PROVIDING FOSTER CARERS AND THEIR FAMILIES WITH SUPPORT

Facilitating peer support

The supervising social worker can provide a carer in their first year of fostering with significant support by linking them with a buddy foster carer. The buddy should be an experienced carer – for example, a carer who has a similar approval category or family structure to the new foster carer. This means that the buddy may have faced some of the same concerns as the new foster carer during their first few placements and may be able to offer them advice, particularly during weekends and evenings when social work support may not be so readily available. The buddy may also be able to take the new foster carer to a support group and introduce them to other carers. New foster carers often find it easier to ask buddies questions about what to expect from their placements and request support from them, particularly if they feel that the concerns they have are minor.

> **The Mockingbird Programme**
>
> This model of support for foster carers was introduced in the UK by the Fostering Network in 2015, under licence from the Mockingbird Society in the US. The aim of the project is to replicate extended family support networks by bringing together six to ten "satellite" fostering households, with a "hub home" operated by an experienced foster carer, supported by a social worker. The hub home offers support, guidance and training to the foster carers, and planned and emergency sleepovers for the children placed in satellite homes. It also organises group activities.
>
> A review of the project undertaken by Ott *et al* for the DfE in 2020 found that the project showed, amongst other positives, 'promising findings around improving well-being for foster carers [and] improving foster carer support' (p 25). Further information about this programme is available from the Fostering Network. Obviously, this programme cannot be established by an individual supervising social worker, as it needs a fostering service to commit to making a change in operating model. However, supervising social workers may find it helpful to consider how the project works and foster carers' perceptions of it. In addition, some concepts from the scheme could be adapted to how peer support is used for carers, such as buddy foster carers being the providers of regular sleepovers for the children of the carers with whom they are buddied.

Introducing foster carers to support groups

Many fostering services require their carers to attend support groups regularly. Not only can participating in these groups enable carers to support each other, but the groups can also be used by the fostering service as vehicles for raising issues relating to all foster carers and providing carers with information about service policies or changes to legislation. It can be daunting for a new foster carer to join an established support group. Therefore, the supervising social worker needs to ensure that the carer understands the group's purpose, and should facilitate their introduction to it, perhaps by accompanying them to a first session and introducing them to other carers, or by arranging for a buddy foster carer to do this. Often, support groups include a learning/training element that can be useful to new carers and provide evidence for their training records.

Supporting other children in the foster home

It important to remember that fostering will result in changes to family life, not only for the foster carers but also for any other children in the household, whether they are full-time residents or, for example, children who live elsewhere but who visit at weekends and during holidays. The impact on the children of the foster family may be positive, as they may forge strong links with the children joining their family. However, the presence of more children in the household could also mean that they have less individual time with their parents.

The lives of the children in the foster family may be impacted by changes in household rules and norms to comply with safe caring policies, and they may be considered by their foster carer parents to be role models for the fostered children, an ideal that is not always easy to live up to. They may witness children being abusive to their parents or behaving in a way they themselves would not be allowed to, and their belongings may also be taken or damaged. Foster children may have an impact on the children of the foster family's friendship groups or sibling relationships, and the dynamics of these relationships may change as a result. The foster family's children may also feel profound loss when a foster child moves on.

The other children in the foster family will experience major changes in their lives through being involved in fostering, so they need to be considered and supported from the moment that the foster carers are approved. Their support needs will vary depending on their age and unique situations.

Höjer *et al*'s journal paper, 'The impact of fostering on foster carers' children: an international literature review', concluded that:

- involving the foster carers' children 'in the decision to foster enhances subsequent adaptation';
- keeping the foster carers' children 'informed about fostering and each particular child reduces conflicts';
- 'foster carers need to identify "protected" time for their children';
- some children of foster carers would rather only have limited information (including limited sensitive information) about the children placed with their family;
- when foster carers' children are 'allowed to discuss openly perceived difficulties with fostering' with their parents and social workers, it improves their 'capacity to cope';
- 'preparing carers' children for the ending of placements' is important (2013, p 19).

Therefore, the supervising social worker should consider how each child in the household can be supported individually. Services have successfully used the following initiatives to support children within foster families:

- providing them with regular individual sessions with the supervising social worker;

- encouraging the foster carer to have protected time with their child;

- enabling the young person to contact the supervising social worker if a situation arises with which they need help;

- linking them with a buddy – a child from an experienced foster family;

- encouraging them to attend groups for the families of foster carers;

- inviting them to a virtual group for the children of foster carers;

- allowing them to join part of their parent's supervision sessions (this option is more suitable for teenagers or young adults, and needs careful consideration to ensure that confidentiality for the foster child is maintained);

- offering them the opportunity to attend family group meetings of the whole household, which are facilitated by the supervising social worker.

In addition, the Fostering Network celebrates carers' children via Sons and Daughters Month, which takes place annually in October. They have created podcasts, certificates and letters that fostering services can use and adapt.

Supporting family and friends carers

Careful thought needs to be given to ensuring that family and friends carers understand why they need to meet the fostering standards. They are often assessed as foster carers during times of family crisis, and frequently in a shorter than usual timescale. Therefore, they may not have had the same opportunities as non-connected applicants to consider the requirements of foster caring and its demands on their time, or the training and development requirements involved. They may well identify themselves by their relationship with the child (e.g. a grandparent) rather than in the role of a professional foster carer, and may need time to adjust to what is being asked of them, and to appreciate the benefits of the training and support available to them.

The supervising social worker could help a family and friends carer by pairing them with a mentor who is an experienced kinship carer, and/or by introducing them to a dedicated support group for family and friends carers, where they can gain knowledge from the experiences of other foster carers in their position.

SUMMARY

Induction for foster carers takes time, but skilful input from the supervising social worker at the start of a carer's fostering career and the establishment of a support package for all members of the fostering family can provide the scaffolding necessary for new foster carers to become successful fostering households.

The next chapter continues to explore the supervising social worker's role in supporting the development of foster carers by discussing the review process.

Chapter 6
Reviews

Once a supervising social worker has established a working relationship with a foster carer and ensured that their induction has been completed, they must help the foster carer to understand fostering processes. One of the key requirements is that foster carers undergo reviews.

WHY FOSTER CARER REVIEWS ARE NEEDED

Regulation 28 of the Fostering Services (England) Regulations 2011 requires fostering services to carry out reviews of all fostering households. All first reviews of fostering households must be presented to the service's fostering panel for their consideration, and each of these must take place one year after the foster carer's approval at the latest. Subsequent reviews should occur when the service considers them to be necessary, such as when changes take place in the foster home or when allegations have been made against the foster carer, but always at intervals that are not greater than one year.

In her guide to foster carer reviews (2015), Cosis Brown highlights some case reviews in which significant events had taken place in foster families that should have triggered foster carer reviews. She is clear that 'this requires those responsible for the supervision of foster carers to assess what change of circumstance or event should trigger the need for an additional or early review' (p 31).

The purpose of a review is to consider the foster carer's ability to continue to meet the NMS, to reflect on their fostering over the preceding time period, and to identify their future training and development needs. This means that the supervising social worker must provide an ongoing assessment of a foster carer's skills and abilities based on all available evidence. This will include information that they have obtained during supervision sessions, from observations in the foster home, and from the children and young people placed, as well as other professionals.

PREPARING REVIEW PAPERWORK

Cosis Brown (2015) and Adams (2019b) have written extensively about the process of preparing for and undertaking a foster carer review. However, in summary, for each review, the supervising social worker should prepare a written report containing:

- a brief summary of the foster household and any changes that have occurred during the review period;
- an overview of the placements that the carer has undertaken that year;
- the fostering skills demonstrated by the carer and their areas of challenge;
- any updates on the carer's health;
- details of unannounced visits that have taken place and any issues that were identified as a result of them;
- the carer's ability to meet the NMS, including:
  - meeting the child's health needs;
  - understanding child development;
  - using effective communication skills;
  - safeguarding;
  - promoting a positive identity;
- details of any complaints or allegations and their outcomes;
- a review of any training undertaken by the carer and any training needs that have been identified;
- the carer's progress on the TSD standards, if applicable;
- the views of the children in placement;
- the views of the carer's own children, if applicable;
- if possible, the views of birth parents of children placed;
- the views of any child's social worker or independent reviewing officer (IRO) involved with children placed with the carer;
- the views of the carers.

The supervising social worker should also write a concluding statement summarising the foster carer's strengths and vulnerabilities, and either recommending that their approval should remain as it is or that specific changes should be made.

It would be helpful for the worker to detail the carer's occupation and working hours, the involvement of any adult children in the household, and any specific needs that any of the foster carer's own children have that may impact on the time that the carer has available for fostering. This is particularly useful when the review is going to be presented to the fostering panel, as it helps to provide a holistic view of the household.

It is essential that, when gathering information for a review, the supervising social worker ensures the voices of the children in the household are heard. This applies not only to children in foster care, but also to other children in the house: birth children, adopted children, or those subject to special guardianship orders. They are experiencing the parenting and care that the foster carer is providing, and so are uniquely placed to provide evidence about it. Consulting the foster carer's children also ensures that they feel their views are valued. Höjer *et al* (2013) state that social workers 'need to give carers' children the licence to discuss difficulties', as this 'can make it easier for children and young people to cope and understand their own feelings' (p 20), but equally the children may be able to highlight the positives of what their parent/s offer as foster carers.

Children in the household can be engaged in review preparation through:

- individual discussions with the supervising social worker;
- group discussions;
- the completion of feedback forms and questionnaires;
- text conversations;
- direct work with craft materials/play materials, etc.

The key to obtaining feedback from the children is for the supervising social worker to establish a relationship with each child or young person, so that rapport is created and there is a level of trust between the parties. The worker can encourage this by visiting at times when the children are present in the home, taking the time to engage with them, and demonstrating an interest in them and their lives from the outset.

In the same way, the worker should establish a relationship with the children or young people placed with their foster carers, so that there is a level of trust and the children feel able to comment honestly and openly about their experiences in the foster family.

CHAIRING A REVIEW

While it is common practice in some fostering services for a supervising social worker or their manager to chair their own reviews, good practice would be for the review to be chaired by someone independent of the line management, such as the manager of another fostering team or an Independent Reviewing Officer (IRO), known in some organisations as a Fostering Independent Reviewing Officer (FIRO).

The supervising social worker's report should be shared with the foster carer prior to the formal review meeting in which it will be discussed, so that they can comment and ask any questions they have about the issues raised within it. The report should then be made available to the Chair in advance of the meeting to allow them to prepare for the discussion. The record of the review discussion should be clearly noted by the Chair and, as an outcome of the meeting, a plan for the next review period should be agreed with the carer and supervising social worker. This should clearly detail the tasks to be undertaken, who they are allocated to, and timescales for completion.

If this is a first annual review that is to be presented to the fostering panel, the supervising social worker should provide the relevant review paperwork to the panel administrator in a timely manner, as it needs to be sent to the panel members at least five working days prior to the meeting.

SUPPORTING FOSTER CARERS PRIOR TO FIRST REVIEWS

The fostering panel's task is to consider whether the foster carer continues to be suitable for the role. This can be quite daunting for some foster carers, particularly if they found their approval panel stressful. The supervising social worker should explain the need for the first review to go to the panel at an early stage of the foster carer's induction into fostering, and remind them of this from time to time during the first year. Sometimes, particularly if concerns were raised during their approval panel, foster carers are asked to come for a first review at the fostering panel sooner, for example, after six months, and this may cause additional anxiety. It is important for the supervising social worker to stress to the foster carer that everyone goes to the panel with their first review, and that an additional aim of the panel is to support their development. Another way of looking at annual reviews is to consider them as a celebration of fostering achievements over the year, and this should certainly be part of the review process.

The supervising social worker should explain the purpose of the panel to the foster carer and provide them with information about the people who sit on it and their roles, as well as the process for hearing panel cases. If a leaflet about the panel is available, they should provide a copy. They should also explain that the panel may recommend that the carer undergoes specific training or development that they feel would benefit them, and that they can ask for carers to return to them for further review if they have any concerns that they wish to see addressed.

The worker and carer should be invited to attend the panel. While the carer is not required to do so, the worker should encourage them to attend. The worker could discuss with the panel adviser and Chair whether it is possible for foster carers to attend by video or phone conferencing if this would enable attendance. This may be particularly helpful if the foster carer lives some distance away or would have to make arrangements for the care of foster children in order to attend. If the worker can find a way of facilitating the carer's attendance, they will then be able to fully participate in discussions about their fostering and provide the panel with details of their experiences. In exceptional cases, where foster carers do not feel able to attend, the supervising social worker should encourage them to produce a written account of their views on the reports being presented to the panel or to make a short video presentation, so that this can be shown to the panel members.

It is also good practice for the supervising social worker's manager to attend the fostering panel, and they should always be invited.

THE FOSTERING PANEL

The fostering panel's role is to:

- understand the carer's experiences of their first year in fostering;
- reflect on the carer's skills and abilities;
- make recommendations to the fostering decision-maker as to whether the carer should continue to foster for the service, and whether their terms of approval match their current skills and availability; and to
- quality assure the reviews, including ensuring that:
    - the statutory checks, medicals, health and safety checks, and safer caring policies are up to date;
    - unannounced visits have occurred;
    - all key issues had been fully explored during the review;
    - the review was held within the required timescale;
    - a note is made as to whether the review was chaired by an independent person.

The supervising social worker's role at the fostering panel is to:

- present the fostering service's assessment of the carer;
- support the carer;

- enable the carer to participate fully in any discussions;

- provide any updates on their carer's situation since the report was finalised and distributed; and

- clarify any information contained in the report for the panel, if necessary.

SUBSEQUENT REVIEWS

Not all subsequent reviews need to be presented to the fostering panel. However, good practice would be for the supervising social worker to present their foster carers' reviews to panel every three years to allow for further quality assurance. Some services, whose fostering panels have the capacity, randomly select reviews held at any stage in a carer's fostering career, and quality assure them.

The following reviews should always be presented to the service's fostering panel:

- reviews where significant changes of approval are recommended;

- reviews after significant life events have happened to a carer;

- reviews where changes of approval are recommended but the carer disagrees with the recommendation;

- reviews after safeguarding concerns or concerns about the standard of care being provided by a carer have been raised.

In the first two scenarios, the supervising social worker's role will usually be the same as it is in the presentation of first annual reviews (i.e. providing the written report to the panel, supporting the carer, and ensuring that the carer is able to participate fully in the panel discussions). The worker's role may also be the same in the last two scenarios, but if they and the carer disagree about the recommended terms of approval or the standards of care being offered to children, it may be more difficult, as the carer may not want the worker to support them.

The supervising social worker should always prepare the written review report and participate in the review. They should also attend the fostering panel to respond to any questions about their report and to provide their professional opinion on the issues being discussed. However, it may be appropriate for the service to provide the foster carer with a separate social worker to support them during the meeting, so that they feel able to participate fully. This could be a duty worker from the fostering team or another supervising social worker, whose role would be to ensure that the carer is able to convey the information they wish the panel to know. Alternatively, the carer may choose to bring their own independent support from an organisation such as FosterTalk.

Where the carer is attending the panel because of concerns or allegations, good practice would suggest that a formal investigation should be conducted, and a written report should then be produced and shared with them. If there is a concern that this is a safeguarding issue, a meeting will be convened by the Local Area Designated Officer (LADO) to see if the threshold for a section 47 investigation (child protection investigation) has been met, and to decide how this will be investigated. Whether an investigation is undertaken under the auspices of the LADO or by the fostering service, a foster carer review meeting, chaired by an independent chair, should be convened following its conclusion. During this meeting, the carer's fostering since the last annual review should be considered, including the issues raised in the investigation, so that a holistic assessment of their fostering can be produced. The supervising social worker and the author of the investigation report should present the report and the review documentation to the fostering panel, along with any written representations that the carer wishes to make. Concerns and allegations are discussed further in Chapter 10.

SUMMARY

The supervising social worker can assist their foster carer to have a positive experience at their reviews by encouraging them to participate fully, to be reflective, and to meet all the requirements of being a foster carer, including keeping up to date with their training and development. Training and development are discussed in the following chapter.

Chapter 7
Providing supervision – training and development

Supervising social workers need to ensure that the foster carers they support understand that they are required to undertake training and development. They should also provide the foster carers with support and advice so that they can maximise the benefits from the training and development that they receive. While foster carers throughout the UK are required to undergo training and development, this chapter focuses on the requirements for those working in England.

TRAINING AND DEVELOPMENT REQUIREMENTS FOR FOSTER CARERS

NMS 20 requires that:

...foster carers receive the training and development they need to carry out their role effectively [and that] *a clear framework of training and development is in place for foster carers, and this is used as a basis for assessing foster carers' performance and identifying their training and development needs.*

(DfE, 2011, p 40)

Each foster carer needs to have a Personal Development Plan (PDP) in place. When the carer is first approved, this plan will consist of the mandatory training required by their service. However, as they become more experienced, it will also include any training that the service believes will help the carer to develop more individually targeted skills and knowledge.

The exact nature of the training required and the subjects that it covers varies from service to service. However, most services include training on the following topics in their mandatory programmes:

- safeguarding
- safer care
- first aid

Other subjects that may be included are:

- understanding behaviour
- attachment theory
- child development
- record keeping
- life story work
- satisfying children's health care needs
- supporting children in education
- equality and diversity

Some services also have specific training tailored to the needs of specialist carers, such as parent and child carers, those who look after unaccompanied asylum-seeking young people, and short break carers.

All foster carers are also required to complete the national Training, Support and Development standards at the start of their fostering careers. These are defined in the *Training Support and Development Standards for Foster Care: Guidance for managers, supervising social workers* (DfE, 2012).

The TSD standards provide a national minimum benchmark that set out what all foster carers should know, understand and be able to do within the first 12 months of approval. They are designed to:

- *Ensure that all foster carers receive relevant induction, training and support, and continuing professional development.*
- *Assist managers and supervisors in assessing the skills, knowledge and experience of foster carers and in identifying their training and development needs*

(DfE, 2012, p 3)

The aims of the TSD standards are to:

...provide foster carers with:

- *A clearer understanding of their role.*
- *Greater confidence and clarity.*
- *An outline of essential knowledge and skills.*
- *Recognition for their developing professionalism.*
- *A pathway for learning and development.*

(DfE, 2012, p 4)

Mainstream foster carers are required to complete these within 12 months of being approved, while family and friends carers must complete them within 18 months of being approved. Many fostering services also work with short break carers who provide respite care for children with disabilities. The DfE publishes a separate set of TSD standards for these carers, which they should complete within 12 months of their approval. However, fostering services can, if they prefer, ask their short break carers to complete the mainstream standards instead and give them 18 months to achieve this.

SUPERVISING TRAINING AND DEVELOPMENT IN PRACTICE

Helping foster carers to meet the initial post-approval requirements

Foster carers can find the first year after their approval to be particularly demanding, as they need to complete both the TSD workbook and their service's mandatory training. Ideally, the service's mandatory training programme should be devised to cross-reference the TSD standards. This will help to ensure that all of its foster carers are supported to achieve the best training and development outcomes possible in their first year. Whether this is the case or not, however, the supervising social worker can ease pressure on newly approved foster carers by designing and implementing a well-planned personal training programme, which links the mandatory training to the TSD standards, and shows the carer how the training can inform their thinking about the standards and provide evidence of their development.

The supervising social worker should ensure that they are familiar with all of the service's mandatory training courses and, ideally, have attended them. This will allow them to have informed conversations with the foster carers about the issues covered in the training, and to assess whether the carers have taken the learning on board and are able to apply it effectively in their day-to-day lives. They should also assist the carers by discussing the key topics in the TSD standards to help them understand the concepts involved and how these can be evidenced from their daily fostering activities with any child in placement.

Some services enable groups of new foster carers to undertake their TSD standards training together so that they can support each other. This works particularly well where the foster carers undertook their induction training together, as they have often established trust between each other and feel that they can talk freely.

> **GOOD PRACTICE EXAMPLE**
>
> Some fostering services supply the TSD workbooks to their foster carers as part of their 'Introduction to fostering' training. They encourage prospective carers to begin to complete these prior to approval, using information that they have learned during their induction. They also give the prospective carers the opportunity to discuss issues arising from the TSD standards with others participating in the training. This introduces the concept of continuous learning and development at an early stage of their fostering career.

The supervising social worker can assist the foster carers further by reminding them to refer to the fostering service's handbook or website regularly. They can also recommend books, leaflets, podcasts and websites that contain additional information for carers. It is helpful if services devise lists of training and development resources so that the worker can make these available to carers when they are completing their mandatory training and TSD workbooks.

However, the supervising social worker should also ensure that they are aware of each foster carer's learning style (see Chapter 4), as this will help them to understand the carer's needs and to support them by giving them the most appropriate advice. Some carers may gain more from reading and researching individual topics on their own, rather than attending courses, while others may find that they benefit from receiving training or discussing topics of mutual interest in small groups. The supervising social worker should bear this in mind and endeavour to make allowances for personal learning preferences where possible when preparing or updating each foster carer's Personal Development Plan (PDP).

Facilitating ongoing and additional training and development

Once a foster carer has completed their mandatory training and TSD workbook, the role of the supervising social worker is to encourage their individual development and continued participation in training. They should individualise each carer's PDP to reflect their growing knowledge base and to specify any areas for development that have been identified through the reviewing process. For example, some carers may need to undergo training in order to better understand a specific issue, such as attachment, while it may be appropriate for others to gain skills in preparation for independence. The PDP should be reviewed and updated annually by the supervising social worker in discussion with the foster carer.

The supervising social worker can use supervision sessions to provide one-to-one training and development on subjects of interest to the foster carer, or where it is felt the carer could benefit from gaining further knowledge about a particular topic. The worker could also take a recognised approach to attachment theory, such as the Secure Base approach (discussed in Chapter 4), and explore this with the carer. This may encourage the carer to take that approach in their one-to-one interactions with the children who have been placed with them. The worker could also explain other models based on attachment theory, such as Dan Hughes' PACE (Playfulness, Acceptance, Curiosity and Empathy) model (2006), in relation to the child's specific needs.

It is also important for the worker to ensure that their foster carers understand they may need to update their training for some subjects, such as first aid and safeguarding, every three years. The worker will need to ensure that this updated training happens and maintain the carer's enthusiasm for refreshing their knowledge. They may be able to find a different first aid course to the one the carer undertook previously, or a presenter who covers different issues. Alternatively, they could recommend that the carer attends a training course on a particular aspect of a subject, such as a course on child sexual exploitation or county lines gangs, rather than another broad introduction to safeguarding course. This will encourage the carer to develop a wide knowledge base about the subject. The worker could also boost a carer's personal development by involving them in the development of service policies and procedures, or by asking them to mentor or help to train new carers.

The supervising social worker should also endeavour to identify additional training opportunities for carers. This could be related to the specific needs of a child for whom they are caring, such as a child with a disability or a young person exploring their gender identity, or be related to some of the issues that arise as common factors in many placements, for example, adult mental health or drug and alcohol issues. It is particularly noticeable in parent and child assessment placements that carers need this information and spend substantial periods of time in supervision discussing these topics. In addition, this type of training may also be helpful for carers who need to supervise a child's contact with a parent or explain a parent's situation to a child. Supervising social workers can play an important role by assisting with the design of training programmes for their carers. However, they can also contribute to the service's development by identifying areas where there is a need for new training options for all carers.

Supervising training and development for households with two foster carers

Where there are two foster carers in a household, but one is acting as a primary carer, consideration should be given to how much involvement the secondary carer should have in training. Both foster carers must demonstrate that they have met the TSD standards. Some of the evidence needed for this can be provided jointly but, where this is not possible, each carer must provide individual evidence.

Each service should have a clear policy on how much training both the primary and secondary carers should undertake each year once they have completed their mandatory training, and the supervising social worker should ensure that this is clearly stated on each carer's PDP. Where a secondary carer works long hours, or works away from home, the supervising social worker may need to consider using alternative training methods, such as evening, weekend or virtual training sessions, or online materials. Sometimes, secondary carers can become distanced from fostering; this can have an impact on the fostering family as a whole and may lead to concerns about the care a foster child is receiving if one carer is disconnected. Attending training with other carers is a good way for them to keep connected and up-to-date with developments in fostering.

Supporting family and friends carers/kinship carers

The supervising social worker also needs to consider the specific needs of family and friends carers/kinship carers, many of whom are likely to be grandparents. Some of these carers may not have engaged in formal education for many years, and may need time to adjust to the idea of learning again. The supervising social worker could assist them by spending part of their supervision sessions discussing any training courses that the carers have attended in order to help them consolidate their learning, or by delivering sections of a training package to the carers themselves, so that they can focus the training on carers' particular needs. If the service supports a large number of family and friends carers, it may be a good idea to provide specialist training for these carers via dedicated support groups.

Establishing and nurturing a culture of learning

Finally, the supervising social worker can assist a foster carer's development by thinking of learning in terms of its widest definition, and encouraging them to develop interests in specialist areas. The carer can then share their knowledge with other foster carers and social workers within the service, thus contributing to the development of a learning culture within the organisation. Supervising social workers should also support carers who are studying for qualifications in childcare and other related subjects, by helping them to find and apply for grants, and by ensuring that the carer has protected study time. If they are able to do this, there is potential for them to make an arrangement with the carer that they will share their new knowledge with other members of the service.

> **Possible training and development resources for foster carers**
> - In-house training courses
> - External training courses
> - Literature (books/journals/audio books)
> - DVDs
> - Podcasts
> - Support group discussions
> - Participation in policy groups run by the service
> - Research projects
> - Higher level study
> - Coaching and mentoring
> - Acting as a trainer, mentor or buddy for other foster carers
> - Individual sessions with a psychologist looking at placement issues
> - Attending conferences on fostering
> - Discussions during supervision
> - Observing/shadowing other foster carers
> - Participation in online foster carer communities

While this guide has explored how supervising social workers can establish relationships with their foster carers, put effective supervision strategies in place, and help the carers to prepare for the role in general, they also need to support them prior to and during placements of children. The next chapter considers the functions of the supervising social worker in planning and supporting placements.

Chapter 8
Providing supervision – case management

One of the key functions of a supervising social worker is to support their foster carers so that they can provide good quality placements for children. They should prioritise the needs of these children at all times when assisting the carers to put their care plans into practice. The supervising social worker has a number of specific responsibilities in respect of case management. This chapter covers some of these responsibilities, such as pre-placement preparation and planning, supporting placements, and supporting carers with the ending of placements.

PREPARING FOSTER CARERS FOR A PLACEMENT OF A CHILD

There are several stages to the task of preparing foster carers for a placement of a child. Firstly, the supervising social worker must ensure that they are fully aware of the foster carer's skills and abilities, as well the areas in which they may need further development. This will enable the worker to provide the carer with informed advice about potential children and whether these would be good matches for them. This means that, when working with a new foster carer, the supervising social worker needs to be familiar with the carer's Form F assessment report and any issues raised by the fostering panel at the time of the carer's approval, if the worker did not carry out the original assessment. When working with experienced foster carers whom they have not supported before, the supervising social worker should familiarise themselves with the assessment report on the family and the reports from any subsequent reviews. Even if the supervising social worker has been working with a foster family for some time, it can still be useful for them to reread the assessment report and any available reports from subsequent reviews, as doing so will enable them to refresh their knowledge about the family and ensure that they are well placed to identify and address any potential matching issues.

Once a potential child has been identified, the supervising social worker's first tasks are to help the foster family to identify the child's needs from the information provided to them, to consider what information may be missing from the referral, and to ask any questions necessary to ensure that full information about the child has been received. Their role then becomes one of facilitator. They should help the foster family to decide whether this child would be right for their household or whether they will be unable to meet this particular child's needs. By allowing the foster family to consider the possible placement of a child with assistance, rather them telling them what they should do, the supervising social worker can enable them to become more aware of their own strengths and vulnerabilities. This, in turn, will help them to develop as foster carers. The supervising social worker can assist them by asking open-ended questions and highlighting the key aspects of a match, but they should always aim to ensure that the foster family makes each decision themselves.

The supervising social worker should also encourage foster carers who already have a child in placement to consider the likely impact on the first child living with the family of accepting a second child, and how the children's personalities and needs would work together. They should ask the first child in placement's social worker for their views about the matter.

PLACEMENT PLANNING MEETINGS

Placement planning meetings should be held prior to a child or young person being placed with a fostering household or, if this is not possible, within five working days of the child moving in. The purpose of these meetings is to:

- share details about the child's background;
- discuss the child's care plan, medical and educational needs;
- agree the limits of delegated authority for the foster carer;
- discuss the safer caring plan and any risk assessments;
- ensure that a placement agreement has been completed.

These meetings should be attended by the child's social worker, the supervising social worker, the foster carer, any other significant professionals, and the birth parents, where this is feasible and appropriate.

The supervising social worker should ensure that the foster carer receives delegated authority agreements from the child's social worker at the point of placement. These are key documents that capture the agreed understanding about who will make everyday decisions for a child, such as medical consents, consents for social and educational activities, etc. They should be signed documents that can be referred to at any point during placement and should also be reconsidered at each review of the child's care plan. Delegated authority agreements are specific to each child, and reflect their age, legal status and care plan. If these documents have not been provided to the foster carer at the point of placement, the supervising social worker should raise this with the child's social worker as a matter of urgency on behalf of the carer.

The supervising social worker should support the foster carer at the placement planning meeting and encourage them to ask questions. If the carer is going to be able to provide the desired outcomes for a child, they will also need to have detailed information about that child to hand so that they can fully meet their identified needs. The supervising social worker should, therefore, ensure that the foster family receives the relevant documentation prior to, or at the point of, placement. These documents could include:

- a signed placement agreement;
- a placement plan;
- a written history of the child;
- a copy of the child's latest assessment;
- a copy of the child's care plan;
- a clear contact plan;
- a record of delegated authority (signed by those with parental authority) for the child;
- a health plan for the child;
- a document specifying medical consents for this placement;
- a safer care agreement specifically prepared for the child;
- any relevant risk assessments;
- a copy of the latest Personal Education Plan (PEP) for the child;
- a copy of any Education, Health and Care Plan (EHCP) for the child;
- a copy of any current court orders relating to the child;
- a copy of the Child Health Record (blue book or red book);
- details of the child's social worker, that social worker's manager, the emergency duty team contact, the child's school, and the child's GP;
- details of the child's likes and dislikes, as well as any triggers for trauma that are known.

If a child is placed in an emergency or with limited notice, there may not be time for a meeting to be held prior to placement and some of the relevant documentation may not be available to the carer in advance. In such cases, the supervising social worker should provide the carer with a list of the documents mentioned above, so that they can request the provision of these as soon as possible. Additionally, the worker can support the carer by advocating on their behalf with the child's social worker to acquire these documents in a timely manner.

It is equally important for the child being placed to be provided with some information about the fostering household, even if the placement is being made in an emergency. The supervising social worker and the foster carer could usefully create a booklet about the foster home and its residents, which could be provided to children in advance of placements. This should, ideally, include photos of household members, their pets, and the fostering bedroom, so that these seem familiar to the child when they arrive at the foster home. It may be helpful for the supervising social worker to provide a basic outline of a welcome booklet to foster carers, as the content and quality of these documents can vary from basic to very detailed documents (which sometimes contain too much information for a child or young person to absorb as an introduction). Good practice would be for the booklet to be regularly updated (and at least annually as part of the annual review process) and for the supervising social worker to store the latest version electronically so they can provide a copy to a child's social worker at the point of placement.

Some foster carers are now imaginatively putting together short videos for children. They have used ideas such as searching for a pet in all rooms in the house and in the garden, which allows the child to have a virtual tour of the property, or filming their own children welcoming the child who is going to be placed and talking about their home. All of these approaches are positive ways of providing a child with information about the home they are going to be moving to.

When children are placed with family and friends carers, the supervising social worker should never assume that the carers know everything about the child. Whilst they may be familiar with some aspects of the child's family history, there may have been breakdowns in family relationships leading to temporary estrangements, so their knowledge may not be up to date. Family members may have concealed some situations from their relatives, and the prospective carers may not be aware of some of the child's health issues or educational needs. Therefore, the worker should ensure that family and friends placements are always made in the same way as unconnected foster carer placements, and that full written information is provided to the carers involved.

Children are often placed with family and friends carers following viability assessments under regulation 24 of the Care Planning, Placement and Case Review Regulations (England) 2010. Technically, a viability assessment demonstrates that there is potential for a placement that requires further assessment. However, services tend to place the child and then complete the assessment later. This often means that a foster carer does not have a supervising social worker at the point of the child's placement. While their assessing social worker may provide them with the relevant information, the supervising social worker, when appointed, should review the information that the family and friends carer has received to ensure that it is comprehensive, and endeavour to provide them with anything that is missing.

Where information or documentation has not been received in a timely manner, the supervising social worker should request this from the child's social worker as a matter of urgency, whether they are working with family and friends or non-connected foster carers.

BRIDGING THE GAP BETWEEN FOSTER CARERS AND OTHER PROFESSIONALS

The previous section explored how a supervising social worker can advocate for a foster carer with a child's social worker in order to ensure that the carer receives relevant written information about a child who is being placed with them. This is just one example of how a supervising social worker can support a foster carer by enabling them to work effectively with other professionals involved in a child's care.

One of the supervising social worker's key roles is to provide a link between the foster carer and the professionals involved in providing childcare services. Usually, there is a wide range of professionals working together to produce and implement a child's care plan, and it is not unusual for newly approved carers to remark on the number of people involved in the care planning for a child. These may include:

- the child's social worker;
- an Independent Reviewing Officer (IRO);
- a nurse for looked after children (LAC nurse);
- a medical adviser;
- a court guardian;
- court-appointed experts;
- CAMHS staff;
- fostering support workers;
- family support workers; and
- virtual school.

The supervising social worker can assist the foster carer by establishing which professionals are working with the placed child, sharing that information with the carer, and explaining the role played by each professional. They should also explain whether these professionals will be in direct contact with the foster carer, or whether they will communicate with them via the child's social worker or formal planning meetings. Where appropriate, the supervising social worker should facilitate introductions to the professionals involved.

The virtual school link is an important professional relationship for both the supervising social worker and the foster carer. The virtual school can take the lead in resolving issues that might have a substantial impact on a child's time with their carer, such as addressing the issue of finding a suitable school placement in a timely manner, dealing with exclusions, etc. This can help the supervising social worker to ensure that the educational part of the child's care plan is being met to a high standard, increasing the stability of the child's placement.

Supervising social workers who are based in independent fostering services may find it challenging to perform these tasks, as they will usually need to establish effective communication channels with the child's social worker in order to receive the information and regular updates that they require. It is often simpler for supervising social workers who are working within the placing local authority, as they may have better access to the child's social worker and the child's history.

It is also important for the supervising social worker to ensure that the foster carer knows when to contact them, when to contact the child's social worker, and which information needs to be shared with both workers. These details should be included in the placement agreement. However, the supervising social worker may, at times, need to help the carer to understand why a child's social worker is making a particular request of them, particularly if they are unhappy about what they are being asked to do. They may also have to explain to a child's social worker why a carer is unhappy about fulfilling a request that they have made.

On occasions when the foster carer and the child's social worker have different views on a matter, the supervising social worker should advocate for the carer by ensuring that their voice is heard, but also should negotiate a solution that works for all parties. Contact plans are frequently sources of tension, as the needs of placed children and their birth families sometimes conflict with the needs of foster families. This may be because contact is being organised for several days a week after school hours or at weekends, which limits the opportunities for the foster family to spend time participating in family activities. There are arguments to support both positions here, as it is important for a child to maintain their family relationships where possible but also to fully experience family life in their foster home. Here, the supervising social worker needs to ensure that they have full information, that they share this with all parties involved, and that they use their negotiation skills to arrive at a positive solution. The supervising social worker can assist by clearly explaining to the child's social worker any reasons why the carer may be resisting the contact plan, and by explaining to the carer why the child's social worker might be advocating it. If there is a court order for contact, both parties must abide by this. However, everyone involved should consider the level and frequency of contact required at the point of placement, so that they have a clear understanding of any issues that could arise. The details of the contact plan can be discussed at court, if necessary, in order to arrive at the best possible outcome for the child and, wherever practicable, to enable the needs of all parties to be met.

Some services have now introduced the concept of resolutions meetings to address such issues. All relevant parties attend these meetings in order to resolve any potential conflicts at an early stage and to avoid situations escalating. Participating in resolutions meetings can be a positive experience, as the attendees are able to focus on one key issue and look for compromise and agreement in the child's best interests.

During a discussion with the author, supervising social workers in an independent fostering service highlighted that they need to liaise regularly with placing fostering services, as they are not party to any day-to-day planning or changes made to the child's care plan, and must ensure that they and their carer are fully informed at all times. They also noted that they need to be vigilant to ensure that their foster carers are not being asked to undertake tasks outside of their placement contracts. When a child is placed in an independent fostering placement, they, as supervising social worker, may have the most contact with that child and the greatest knowledge of the current situation and issues. However, they have no say in the decisions being made about the care planning, and they found this to be frustrating at times.

It may be appropriate for the child's social worker and the supervising social worker to commit to communicating regularly at the point of placement, or to undertaking periodic joint visits to the foster carer, and for this to be included in the written placement agreement to ensure that it occurs. The supervising social worker's aim should be to ensure that information flows smoothly between the foster carer and the child's social worker, so that the child's care plan can be delivered effectively. Children's social workers frequently have full caseloads and sometimes inadvertently fail to provide foster carers with relevant and up-to-date information about the children placed with them. The example above of advocating with the child's social worker to provide relevant written information at the point of placement is just one example of how a supervising social worker can help their carers to engage with other professionals working with a child.

Children's Looked After reviews

The supervising social worker can also facilitate discussion and information exchange between the foster carers and professionals by participating in the children's Looked After reviews in order to clarify information and contribute to the continued development of the care plan. Unfortunately, supervising social workers in some services are not automatically invited to these reviews, but this could be discussed at the placement planning meeting to ensure that their desire to be involved and support their foster carer is known.

> **Me and My World Reviews**
>
> Some local authorities refer to Looked After reviews by other names. For example, in Brighton and Hove, the process is known as a "Me and My World Review". This local authority makes it clear that these reviews form part of a process, rather than being one-off events. During the reviews, focus is placed on ensuring that the child knows their history, is aware of their progress, and is able to recognise and celebrate their achievements. The supervising social worker is involved in this process and will discuss any issues that arise during it with the foster carer and other professionals. They will then come to an agreement as to whether these issues should be raised in the meeting or discussed separately so the focus of the meeting is on the child's key achievements.
>
> (Brighton and Hove City Council, undated)

Information sharing at the point a child's placement ends

In order to bridge the gap between foster carers and other professionals, and strengthen these relationships, it is good practice for the supervising social worker to ascertain the views of the professionals involved in a child's placement when it reaches an end. Children's social workers' views on placements during the last 12 months are sought as part of the annual foster carer review process, but the response rate for these requests is normally quite low. If a supervising social worker asks for a child's social worker and other professionals to express their views at the point when the placement ends, these professionals' memories of the placement will still be fresh. Therefore, the worker and carer may be able to reflect on their responses, in order to inform the carer's future practice.

Providing foster carers with information about service decisions and changes

The supervising social worker must always bear in mind the need for information to flow smoothly between the carer and the fostering service. This also means communicating with the carer when the service is making any changes to that carer's terms and conditions of engagement. The worker should ensure that the relevant information is delivered clearly, and in a way that means the carer can hear and understand the reasons for decisions being made, even if they do not agree with them. In order to perform the role successfully, the supervising social worker needs to:

- act as an information conduit;

- help the carer to understand changes in service policies and procedures;

- help the carer to find out about and be able to access training opportunities;

- enable the carer to take advantage of any social networking opportunities that are available.

The supervising social worker is also the means by which the foster carer's lived experience of fostering and of particular placements can be fed back to the fostering service and influence its development.

One of the key causes of conflicts between services and their carers is the alteration of the foster carer banding and payment systems. The supervising social worker can often find themselves on the receiving end of their foster carer's dissatisfaction when this happens. In such cases, the worker should ensure that there is an exchange of information between the carer and the fostering service, and facilitate this when necessary. They should ensure that the carer receives a clear explanation of the reasons for the proposed changes, both verbally and in writing, and that they are told how they can make representations about the changes to the service if they wish to do this. The worker can also refer the carer to the fostering handbook or relevant website where appropriate.

Ensuring that foster carers are included as professionals in key meetings

Foster carers live with the children placed with them 24 hours a day, seven days a week, and therefore quickly come to understand each child and their needs. It is important, therefore, that every professional involved in a child's care acknowledges that the foster carer is a key professional who has significant information to share and who can make valuable contributions to the care planning meetings and reviews that take place in respect of that child.

The supervising social worker's role here is to advocate for the foster carer's inclusion in all key meetings. Where possible, they should accompany the carer to these meetings and ensure that their voice is given equal weight to the voices of the other professionals in the room. It may be helpful for the supervising social worker to help the carer to make notes prior to the meeting, detailing the issues that they wish to raise, or to help them to prepare a written report for the other professionals who will be attending. This can boost the carer's confidence, making it simpler for them to present the information they have to their fellow meeting participants.

This concept of the foster carer as a professional "expert" is one that the supervising social worker can embed throughout their service. In some local authorities, supervising social workers take part in induction sessions for newly qualified social workers and those joining the authority from elsewhere to talk about the role that the foster carer plays in achieving outcomes for children, and to emphasise the experience and knowledge that many carers have. This can help to nurture positive working relationships between social workers and foster carers, and this, in turn, can benefit the children in placement.

DIRECT INVOLVEMENT WITH THE CHILD IN PLACEMENT

Whilst the primary responsibility for working with a child in placement lies with the child's social worker, the supervising social worker will always have direct contact with that child. In fact, when a child is in a long-term or permanent placement, the supervising social worker may visit the household frequently while the child's social worker visits less often.

It is perfectly appropriate for the supervising social worker to form a relationship with a child or young person in placement, as long as they remain conscious that the child's social worker is responsible for their care planning. This will also help when the supervising social worker is having reflective discussions with a foster carer about how they are managing the child's therapeutic care needs. In fact, if they are able to build a strong relationship with the child, the supervising social worker may be able to assist the carer by explaining complex issues to the child or by supporting the carer to do so. Some services even actively encourage supervising social workers to develop and nurture relationships with the children in placement in their foster families so that they can support their care plans and provide more assistance to the foster carers.

> **GOOD PRACTICE EXAMPLE**
>
> In one fostering service in Devon, a supervising social worker and two social work assistants who support foster carers have been trained to deliver the Duke of Edinburgh's Award scheme to young people placed with their foster carers. The advantages of this include:
>
> - The young people are encouraged to be aspirational.
>
> - The young people gain a recognised award.
>
> - The young people develop positive relationships with fostering service staff.
>
> - The foster carers have some respite while the young people are participating in the scheme's activities.
>
> (Pathway Care, Ashburton, Devon)

SUPPORTING FOSTER CARERS WITH TRANSITIONS

One of a foster carer's most significant tasks is to help the children placed with them to move on. This may happen as part of a rehabilitation plan for the child to return to their birth family, or because the child is moving to a permanent placement, which could be a long-term foster home, an adoptive placement, or a special guardianship arrangement with family members. The issue of endings and disruptions is discussed further in Chapter 10, but here the focus is on supervising foster carers to support transitions. When a child moves on, it can be an emotional experience for the foster carer and their family, as they will have formed a bond with the child. Therefore, the supervising social worker will need to provide them with support so that they can make the transition a positive experience, both for the child and for themselves.

Foster carers will deal with the loss they feel when a child moves on in different ways. Some like to take a break from placements and focus on their own family unit for a while. If they have been looking after a baby, for example, they may want to take some time to enjoy family activities that were not possible with such a young child in the household. Other foster carers prefer to take new placements as soon as possible, in order, perhaps, to distract themselves. While both of these approaches are appropriate, the supervising social worker needs to talk with the family prior to the child moving on about how they may feel when the move happens and how they wish to handle the situation. The worker should make it clear to the carer that it is important for them to acknowledge the loss and to accept that it is usual to have an emotional reaction to a child's move. They should also try to ensure that the carer gives themself the emotional space to deal with their feelings.

Supporting the foster carer can be challenging if they do not agree with the child's care plan. This sometimes happens when a child is being rehabilitated to parents whom the carer does not think are able to meet their needs, or being placed with adopters whom the carer has not managed to form a working relationship with. In such cases, the supervising social worker needs to encourage the carer to realise that, while their feelings are valid and stem from their desire to achieve the best for the child, the fostering service and other childcare workers involved have carefully considered the plan and believe it to be the correct course of action for the child. The supervising social worker needs to allow the carer to share their feelings openly, but should also encourage them to consider the positives they have observed about the family members or new carers, and the child's own response to the plan. In addition, they should ensure the carer understands that the child needs to feel they are supporting the plan. The child may be attuned to the carer's thoughts and feelings and, if they appear to be ambivalent about the new placement, the child will sense it and this may destabilise the placement before it has begun.

> **Tools to help transitions**
>
> To help a foster carer to build a good relationship with the permanent carers and enable a smooth transition to permanent placement for the child, the supervising social worker can:
>
> - encourage the carer to prepare a "day in the life" document for the new carers about the child's routines, likes and dislikes;
>
> - provide the carer with books, DVDs, etc, featuring moving on stories to use with the child;
>
> - suggest that the carer write a personal letter to the child about their memories of them, which can be shared with the young person in later life;
>
> - recommend that the carer prepares a photo album of all the experiences the child had in their foster home;
>
> - facilitate regular discussions between the adults on how introductions are progressing and encourage them to raise any concerns, so that these can be resolved at an early stage;
>
> - talk to the carer about how they will manage farewells and acknowledge their feelings of loss (see Chapter 10 for further advice on this).

Consideration also needs to be given to any children of the foster carer and how they will respond to a child moving on. It would be appropriate for the supervising social worker to undertake some direct work with these children to explain the move and the reasons for it in advance. It may help the foster carer's children to be involved in putting together cards, letters, drawings, or videos for the child who is moving on. They could also offer them some individual sessions following the move to allow them to express their feelings, which may be mixed, particularly if the child who has moved required a lot of their parent's time and attention or presented management issues within the household.

Another task for the supervising social worker may be to clarify, on the foster carer's behalf, whether the child's care plan includes a proposal for any ongoing contact between the carer and the child moving on and, if it does, how that contact will be managed.

The Fostering Network's Keep Connected Principles (available from www.thefosteringnetwork.org.uk) and the Family Rights Group's Lifelong Links project (https://frg.org.uk/lifelong-links/) provide useful information about the importance of former foster carers to children in care and how lifelong links can be promoted.

Moves to family and friends carers

The advice above is equally relevant whether the child is moving from a short-term placement to a permanent fostering or adoption placement, or to a family and friends carer. While the new carers may have a pre-existing relationship with a child, they may not have lived with them for any period of time or cared for them following trauma. Therefore, the supervising social worker should be recommending carefully planned introductions and the provision of life story material to these carers, as they would in any other move to permanency. This ensures that the child and their needs are kept central to everyone's thinking and that they are well supported to make a significant move in their life.

Transitioning to a permanent foster placement within the same foster home

The supervising social worker has a significant role to play when the plan for a child who has been living in a foster home becomes a plan for long-term or permanent fostering, and the carer, or the child's social work team, propose that the child stays permanently with their current carer. The tasks involved include helping the foster carer focus on the impact that this would have on the child, themself and their family members, and their future fostering plans.

The worker should help the carer to separate their emotional responses to the situation from the practical aspects and to consider the issue in a holistic manner. This means posing questions such as:

- Does the family have the physical and emotional space for a young person until they reach the age of 18 and beyond?
- Are they able to meet this young person's needs in the long term?
- Have they considered the views of family members?
- What are the future challenges likely to be?
- Are they able to deliver all aspects of the young person's care plan?
- Are they able to meet the requirements of any contact plan?
- Are they approved to take permanent placements and, if not, are they likely to be approved?
- Are they prepared to offer Staying Put (a form of transition discussed in more detail below)?

There will be occasions when a foster family wishes to offer a permanent placement but the child's care plan means that this is not possible. In such cases, the supervising social worker will need to help the carer to manage their own strong feelings while moving the child on to the agreed placement. This usually requires several visits to allow the carer to share their understandably emotional response to the situation and to reassure them that they are heard and empathised with, before it is then possible to go over the reasons for the decisions and prepare the carer for supporting the child to move on.

Staying Put

Staying Put is a form of transition that supervising social workers need to assist foster carers to plan for and adapt to. While there have always been young people who remained with their foster carers after their 18th birthdays on an informal basis, the Children and Families Act 2014 formalised this as a "Staying Put" arrangement. This legislation requires local authorities to facilitate, monitor and support these arrangements until the young person reaches the age of 21, unless the local authority considers that the Staying Put arrangement is not consistent with the young person's welfare.

This can be described as a transition because it is not an extension of a fostering arrangement. It is, instead, a new arrangement between the young person and the foster carer, where fostering regulations, statutory guidance and NMS no longer apply.

The role of the supervising social worker here is to work with the foster carer at an early stage in any possible planning for a Staying Put placement, and to consider the full implications of the transition from a fostering arrangement to this new agreement.

> **Staying Put placements**
>
> When planning for a possible Staying Put placement, the supervising social worker should:
>
> - Discuss the possible implications for the fostering household with the foster carer, including:
>   - any potential impact on fostering approval due to capacity in the household;
>   - the fact that regulations, etc, no longer apply;
>   - the need for a written placement agreement between the young person and the carer;
>   - any support that the carer would need from the local authority;
>   - the financial implications of a possible placement on the foster family, including any impact that it would have on benefits or tax liabilities that might arise.
>
> - Consider convening a foster carer review, as Staying Put constitutes a major change to a foster home. The transition would mean that another adult is present in the home, which could affect other foster placements.
>
> - Liaise with the young person's social worker or personal adviser, the foster carer and the young person to negotiate a placement agreement.
>
> - Arrange for a DBS check to be completed in respect of the young person as an adult within the foster home.
>
> - Ensure that the correct financial arrangements are in place for the carer.
>
> - Ensure that any agreed support services are in place.
>
> - If the carer is continuing to foster, include training that might enhance their skills in providing Staying Put care when devising their PDP.
>
> - Ensure that the young person who is Staying Put is discussed in reviews and supervision sessions when working with other children being fostered in the home.

It is important to note that a Staying Put situation may have different financial implications for a family and friends carer than it does for a non-related foster carer. Young people "Staying Put" with non-related foster carers are able to claim the housing element of Universal Credit. However, this is not payable to young people staying with former foster carers who are defined as close relatives, such as brothers, sisters or step-parents. It can be payable to young people residing with grandparents or aunts and uncles provided that there is a clear contract for accommodation in place.

Further information about the key issues to be considered in a Staying Put discussion can be found in *Staying Put: A good practice guide* (Children's Partnership, 2014), which is available on the Fostering Network and Fosterline websites.

SUPPORTING FOSTER CARERS TO MANAGE CHALLENGING BEHAVIOUR

A key task for supervising social workers is to support foster carers to care for children with troubled/troubling behaviour. Ideally, they should provide their foster carers with information about possible issues before they occur, so that the carer is aware of the signs, can look out for further indicators, and knows they can discuss their concerns openly with their worker. This means building a relationship of trust, and ensuring that carers have access to training and other learning resources to constantly update their knowledge.

Troubled/troubling behaviour can manifest in a range of ways:

- Loss of temper and loss of control
- Being withdrawn and uncommunicative
- Being economical with the truth
- Taking other people's possessions
- Hoarding of food
- Running away from the foster home
- Lack of empathy for others
- Aggression
- Anxiety
- Cruelty to animals
- Incontinence
- Soiling or smearing faeces
- Sexualised behaviour

- Vulnerability to gang culture
- Vulnerability to radicalisation
- Vulnerability to sexual exploitation
- Developing depression or anxiety
- Self-harm

The supervising social worker's role in this situation is to give the foster carer the time and space to:

- explore the issues involved;
- identify the behaviour that they are concerned about;
- reflect on the child's life experiences and consider how these might have led to the identified behaviour;
- assess whether it is the right time to try to address and change that behaviour;
- consider whether there are other aspects of the child's current needs that take precedence over this.

This decision as to whether or not to address the behaviour will be influenced by whether that behaviour puts the child or another person at risk. The foster carer may also need some support to reflect on the fact that the child may not have the language or ability to convey the emotions or difficulties that they are experiencing. The behaviour may be the child's way of communicating their distress or concerns.

In *Managing Difficult Behaviour* (2015), Pallet *et al* highlight how a foster carer's state of mind can influence how they view a child's behaviour. They point out that a child's behaviour could make a carer feel 'angry and hostile to the child', or might leave the carer feeling 'hopeless and demoralised'. They add that the carer may experience thoughts such as 'He takes no notice of what I say, everyone walks over me. I have no authority' (p 18).

The supervising social worker should encourage the foster carer to consider their own level of reflective functioning here. Reflective functioning is explained in the introduction to the University College London (UCL) online Reflective Functioning Questionnaire as 'the capacity to understand ourselves and others in terms of intentional mental states, such as feelings, desires, wishes, goals and attitudes' (https://www.UCL.ac.uk).

In their journal paper, 'Foster carers' reflective understandings of parenting looked after children: an exploratory study' (2015), Bunday *et al* discuss how the parent figure 'needs to understand the complex interplay between their own feelings (mental states) and the child's inner experience' (p 146). They add that, 'It is conceivable that without the capacity to find emotional meaning in a child's behaviour, foster carers will be unable to offer a flexible repertoire of responses' (p 147).

This theme was further developed by Redfern *et al* (2018), when devising their Reflective Fostering Programme. This is a group-based programme for foster carers of children aged 4–11, which aims to develop foster carers' reflective functioning and support the relationships between foster carers and the children in their care.

Group training of this kind is valued by foster carers. In fact, Octoman and McLean (2013) found that foster carers identified it as one of the most popular methods by which to access support (p 154).

However, supervising social workers can also focus on a carer's reflective functioning in individual support sessions. For example, Bunday *et al* (2015) suggested that, when a child becomes angry, the following questions could be posed in order to explore the foster carer's understanding of a child's mental state:

> *Describe a time in the last week when you and (your child) really "clicked" and a time in the last week when you weren't "clicking".*
>
> *How do you think (your child) felt?*
>
> *When your child is upset, what does he/she do?*
>
> *How does this make you feel? What do you do?*
>
> (pp 156–157)

This encourages the carer to focus on the emotions behind the behaviour, and also allows them to reflect on their own thoughts and actions.

Once the supervising social worker has enabled the carer to focus on the emotions that they and the child are experiencing, they could discuss various behaviour management techniques. These include those found by Pallett *et al* (2015), who draw on the Maudsley Hospital Fostering Changes programme, and recommend approaches such as:

- Modelling the desired behaviour
- Using praise to shape behaviour
- Using play to promote positive relationships
- Using rewards
- Using selective ignoring
- Setting limits

The supervising social worker can help the foster carer to reframe their response and to consider the child's behaviour from a different perspective in supervision. They should enable the carer to see that the behaviour is not targeted at the carer directly/personally, and help them to find an alternative way of viewing the behaviour that will allow them to deal with the issue constructively.

Many fostering services offer their foster carers training in Dyadic Developmental Psychotherapy (DDP) to enable them to help a child recover from early childhood trauma. This practice involves relationship-focused treatment based on attachment theory, and supervising social workers can assist carers to implement strategies developed from this training by discussing the principles regularly during supervision.

Supervising social workers can also facilitate discussions at support groups about ways in which other carers have addressed different behaviours, arrange specific training for carers, or recommend literature about managing behaviour.

Another model of support with effective results is where foster carers can access therapeutic parenting courses, usually facilitated by specialist children in care psychologists.

> **Managing behaviour: further resources**
>
> Useful literature for foster carers includes:
>
> Pallet C *et al* (2015) *Managing Difficult Behaviour: A handbook for foster carers of the under 12s*
>
> Butler J (2009) *Behaviour*
>
> Naish S (2018) *The A–Z of Therapeutic Fostering: Strategies and solutions*
>
> Hughes D (2009) *Attachment-Focused Parenting: Effective strategies to care for children*
>
> Elliott A (2013) *Why Can't My Child Behave? Empathetic parenting strategies that work with adoptive and foster families*
>
> Morgan N (2013) *Blame my Brain: The amazing teenage brain revealed*
>
> Bond H (2020) *The Foster Carer's Guide to Parenting Teenagers*
>
> www.nspcc.org.uk: The NSPCC's website includes information to help carers understand and approach a range of issues, including self-harm, drug and alcohol abuse, and child exploitation.
>
> www.familylives.org.uk: Advice on how to tackle a host of issues, including drug use and underage drinking.

> **Issue-based resources**
>
> **Self-harm and addiction**
>
> *Don't Lose the Head:* A support booklet for parents and carers dealing with issues of drugs and alcohol. Produced by CrossCare and available from www.drugs.ie.
>
> www.youngminds.org.uk: A UK charity dedicated to improving children and young people's mental health.
>
> www.talktofrank.com: Information and advice about drugs and alcohol.
>
> www.familylives.org.uk: Advice on how to tackle drug use and underage drinking, as well as a host of other issues.
>
> www.priorygroup.com: Contains information about mental health and addiction issues.
>
> **Exploitation and radicalisation**
>
> For some foster carers, the issues they may be dealing with could include child sexual exploitation, gang culture and crime, and radicalisation. Fostering services are now creating their own training courses to prepare carers to address these challenges, but here are some additional sources of information.
>
> Bond H (2021) *Things Foster Carers Need to Know*: series of five pamphlets providing information on internet safety, self-harm, sexuality, radicalisation, and gangs.
>
> Fursland E (2017) *Caring for a Child who has been Sexually Exploited*
>
> www.gov.uk: The Home Office's website includes advice about gangs and the criminal exploitation of children for parents and carers.
>
> www.childrenssociety.org.uk: Provides information and advice for both professionals and young people on a range of topics, including child sexual exploitation.
>
> www.nationalcrimeagency.gov.uk: Includes information about the criminal and sexual exploitation of children.
>
> www.internetmatters.org: Includes information to help families to protect children from online dangers, including radicalisation and grooming.

The supervising social worker can help the foster carer to access these resources, and then discuss their concerns and the possible approaches they can adopt to address the issues they are experiencing. However, where there are serious concerns, they need to ensure that the carer is not trying to address them on their own and that all the key professionals are involved. They will need to liaise with the child's social worker to ensure that they are aware of the behavioural concerns. They should then ensure that they, the child's social worker and the carer address the issue together. Where there is a significant safeguarding issue, they may need to request a formal risk assessment meeting or a Child Sexual Exploitation assessment.

ASSISTING FOSTER CARERS TO ASSESS OUTCOMES FOR CHILDREN

The Oxford Learner's Dictionary defines an outcome as 'the result or effect of an action or event'. When children are accommodated and placed in foster care, services endeavour to measure the outcomes from these actions. Any foster carer undertaking the care of a child may be asked to contribute to a discussion about the outcomes that have been achieved as part of the review of the child's care plan.

When a foster carer is engaged in the day-to-day tasks that need to be performed when caring for a traumatised child, they can find it hard to be able to see that the child is achieving positive outcomes, and to recognise that taking even a small developmental step can be a huge achievement for a child. The supervising social worker should help the carer to understand that they may be able to identify positive outcomes for children who have experienced poor parenting and home conditions in a range of areas. For example, they might be able to see improvements in the child's:

- physical health
- mental health
- school attendance
- educational achievements
- behaviour
- ability to form attachments
- ability to make and sustain friendships
- ability to develop resilience
- ability to engage in extra-curricular activities
- self-image
- confidence

In Chapter 4, consideration was given to using a strengths-based approach when supervising a foster carer. We also examined how the supervising social worker could explore this with the carer in order to encourage them to use this approach with any child in their care. This can be particularly useful as a mechanism for encouraging a carer to focus on positive outcomes for the children placed with them.

The supervising social worker should encourage the carer to focus on the child's current strengths, abilities and skills during discussions about outcomes, rather than on any concerns they have about the child or negative behaviours that the child is displaying. They should also ask the carer to reflect on any changes that have occurred in these areas of development since the child was placed in their care. The carer may then be able to identify outcomes that have been achieved and the steps that were taken in order to reach these. This could make it easier for them to help the child to achieve additional positive outcomes in future.

All in all, the supervising social worker's role in terms of case management is to ensure that each foster carer is well-prepared for placements, advocated for, guided, and well supported, so that the children in their care can achieve the best outcomes possible. As part of this, they must also ensure that their foster carers are culturally competent. The next chapter investigates what this means and how foster carers can achieve this.

Chapter 9
Providing supervision – cultural competency

Foster carers are required to care for children from diverse backgrounds, and fostering services need to be assured that their carers value each child as a unique individual and respect their ethnic, cultural and religious background. For the supervising social worker, this means ensuring that the foster carers they supervise are culturally competent. This chapter explores the meaning of the term "cultural competency", and how supervising social workers can support foster carers to work in a culturally-competent way.

Cross *et al* (1989, p 13) defined cultural competency as:

> ...a set of congruent behaviours, attitudes, and policies that come together in a system, agency, or among professionals and enable that system, agency, or those professionals to work effectively in cross-cultural situations.

This definition still holds true today.

Social care workers can be regarded as being culturally competent if they approach people from different cultures than their own with an open manner, show them respect and have a desire to learn about their culture. They also need to differentiate some of the services that they provide to meet the needs of individuals, as opposed to taking a "culturally blind" approach and providing the same service to everyone, whatever their culture, religion, ethnicity, gender, sexual orientation or disability.

In order for an organisation to be culturally competent, those working for it need to be aware of their own beliefs and values, and be prepared to challenge themselves and others to aid personal development in this area. For supervising social workers working with foster carers, this may mean helping the carers to explore their own beliefs and values. They may need to encourage some carers to name and discuss these beliefs and values, as they may not have considered this area of self-awareness in detail before. Other carers, meanwhile, may have high levels of self-awareness in relation to their everyday lives, but need to reflect on the impact of their beliefs and values on their role as foster carers, and the supervising social worker should help them to do this.

SUPPORTING FOSTER CARERS LOOKING AFTER YOUNG PEOPLE FROM DIFFERENT ETHNICITIES

If fostering professionals are to be culturally competent, they need to be able to care for young people with a range of ethnic origins. This has become even more important recently, as there has been a rise in the number of foster carers offering placements to unaccompanied young people seeking asylum in the UK. Supervising social workers can assist carers to develop expertise in this area of fostering by providing practical support. This could mean:

- ensuring that carers know how to download and use relevant translation apps on their phones and/or computers to enable communication with the young people, or providing access to translators;

- providing carers with information about social groups and religious groups that they or the young people in their care can join, so that they can feel less isolated and build relationships with people in similar positions or from the same culture;

- identifying reputable sources of information about different religions, cultures and refugee support services. It can be useful for the supervising social worker to create a database of these so that carers can access them whenever required.

CoramBAAF has published a range of introductory booklets that may be helpful for foster carers who are caring for unaccompanied asylum-seeking young people, each of which explains the languages, religions, cultures, food and family life within a specific country. These are currently available for Afghanistan, Eritrea, Iraq, Sudan and Vietnam (Fursland, 2020).

The supervising social worker should also endeavour to help the foster carer to understand the reality of being a young person in a different country and culture. This involves highlighting the fact that the young person may feel overwhelmed and confused when their usual points of reference, such as family, language, and customs, are not available. The carer needs to see each young person as an individual and find out which aspects of their own culture they would like to follow and which aspects they feel are negotiable.

In a journal paper published in 2019, titled 'Fostering unaccompanied asylum-seeking young people: the views of foster carers on their development and support needs', Sidery quotes a foster carer looking after a young Muslim man. Having read on the internet that Muslims only eat meat if it is halal, the carer had gone to great lengths to source some (pp 12–13). However, she then discovered that the young person was eating non-halal products when outside the foster home. The carer discussed this with him and discovered that he did not wish to restrict his diet too much (p 13).

Supervising social workers can also help foster carers to consider whether a young person's behaviour relates to their culture or to the experiences they may have had whilst on their asylum journey. Some young people may have been trafficked, for example, or have lived on their own for a long time without parental oversight. The supervising social worker should also encourage foster carers to reflect on the fact that the notion of fostering does not exist in some cultures, and it may take time for a young person to understand the concept and adjust to living in a foster home.

While providing advice and support to foster carers, the supervising social worker should refrain from giving them detailed advice about the asylum process itself. Sidery (2019) found that some social workers had provided foster carers with inaccurate information about the process (p 13). Instead, they should introduce carers to refugee organisations that can support them in this area and help them in respect of any cultural issues that arise.

> **Further information: unaccompanied asylum-seeking children**
>
> These organisations/people may be able to help with issues around unaccompanied asylum-seeking children and young people.
>
> - Refugee Council – www.refugeecouncil.org.uk
> - Coram Voice – www.coramvoice.org.uk
> - The Children's Society – www.childrenssociety.org.uk
> - Refugee Action – www.refugee-action.org.uk
> - Specialist immigration solicitors

Some of the above information is also relevant in cases where a foster carer is looking after a young person from an ethnicity or culture that is different to their own, and who is not an asylum seeker. For example, the supervising social worker should provide the foster carer with advice about where to find cultural links and information. Ideally, the fostering service should consult with the child's birth parents at the point of placement and ask them which aspects of their culture or religion they would like the foster carers to adopt. The supervising social worker should then discuss this with the foster carer so that they can ensure that this occurs, and agreements should be clearly recorded in the placement plan.

If English is not the child or young person's first language, the supervising social worker should work with the foster carer to find ways of helping the child to retain their knowledge of their first language and, therefore, part of their identity. They should also discuss the provision for the child's cultural needs with the carer on a regular basis during supervision sessions.

SUPPORTING A YOUNG PERSON'S CULTURAL IDENTITY

NMS 2.1 requires that 'children are provided with personalised care that meets their needs and promotes all aspects of their individual identity' (DfE, 2011, p 8). In light of this, the supervising social worker should encourage each foster carer they support to gain as much understanding as possible about the young person in their care so that they can meet their specific needs. They should advise the carer to ask the young person about their culture and show a genuine interest in understanding the similarities and differences between their experiences and the child's lived experiences. By doing this, the carer will enable the child to feel that their personal beliefs and life history are acknowledged and valued by them.

The supervising social worker can help the foster carer to "put themselves in the shoes" of the child or young person placed with them. For example, they could ask the carer to imagine how it would feel to be placed in a strange home, where they do not know where to find anything, do not understand the language that the people living with them are speaking, are not sure what beliefs the people looking after them hold, and do not know what the household's rules are. They can then ask the carer to consider what actions they would want the people looking after them to take so that they felt cared for and respected. They could also ask them to identify any actions that a carer might take that would make them feel unwelcome and unsupported.

Additionally, the supervising social worker should ask the foster carer to focus on their own knowledge and understanding of the young person's culture. They can then encourage them to reflect on whether this understanding comes from the young person themselves or, for example, from discussions with other people, books, television, newspapers, or the internet. The carer should consider whether there is any evidence to support the views that they hold, and the worker can highlight any views that appear to be based on a stereotype rather than facts. They can also encourage the carer to ask the young person about their culture and incorporate some of their traditions into the life of the fostering household.

Foster carers may find it easier to help a young person feel comfortable in their home if they role-model their acceptance of diversity on a routine basis. This could mean:

- displaying art, decorations and furnishings from a range of cultures within their home;

- providing household members and guests with ethnically diverse food and drink, some of which the young person may wish to help prepare;

- celebrating a range of different religious and other festivals; and

- promoting a culture of open discussion and challenging any discriminatory comments heard.

Therefore, when undertaking home visits to foster carers, the supervising social worker should consider whether each home reflects an acceptance and promotion of diversity and, if not, what changes could be made within it to ensure that it does.

The supervising social worker should also encourage the foster carer to help children placed with them to retain their cultural identities. They can do this by encouraging the carer to:

- find television programmes or films featuring the child's culture, and watch and discuss these together;

- have artwork or books about the child's culture in the foster home;

- provide ethnically diverse story books, and books in the child's first language;

- provide films or television programmes in the child's first language;

- highlight sports people, music stars or other public figures who share the child's culture and discuss them with the child;

- attend social events linked to the child's culture; and

- build relationships with members of community groups that reflect the child's origins.

The Black Lives Matter movement has highlighted the need to ensure that conversations about race and equality take place in all foster homes and with all looked after children, whether they are from ethnic minorities or not. It also encourages young people to be aware of discrimination, unconscious bias and disadvantage so that they can understand the issues faced by others, and to be aware and reflective in relation to their own behaviour.

Supervising social workers could encourage foster carers to have these conversations with all children in their household.

> **Further resources: racism and Black Lives Matter**
>
> These are a small selection of resources that could help foster carers to engage with racism and issues surrounding the Black Lives Matter movement with their foster children – many more are available.
>
> *Empowering Foster Carers to Discuss Race Inequalities* – This leaflet, published by FosterTalk, is designed to help foster carers to discuss race inequality, racism and privilege with the young people in their care. It is available from www.fostertalk.org.
>
> *A Parent's Guide to Black Lives Matter* – Created by digital home care platform Yoopies, this booklet provides advice and suggestions to help carers to discuss race and the Black Lives Matter movement with young people. It can be downloaded from www.yoopies.co.uk.
>
> *Black Lives Matter* – The Fostering Network's Black Lives Matter website page (www.thefosteringnetwork.org.uk/node/12209) includes details of, and links to, a host of relevant resources, articles, reports, organisations and more.

SUPPORTING FOSTER CARERS WHO ARE LOOKING AFTER LGBTQ+ YOUNG PEOPLE

Cultural competence also applies to caring for young people who define themselves as LGBTQ+.[1] In a paper published in 2019, titled 'Providing a secure base for LGBTQ young people in foster care: the role of foster carers', Schofield *et al* investigated foster carers' experiences of fostering LGBTQ+ young people and used the Secure Base Model to analyse the relationships between the carers and the young people. They concluded that fostering services need to explore their carers' values and attitudes towards LGBTQ+ issues (p 380). This should occur both in the pre-approval assessment and post-approval in supervision, as it is crucial that foster carers accept and value sexual and gender diversity. In addition, they noted that supervising social workers should provide foster carers with post-approval training and support in relation to these issues, including providing information about LGBTQ+ support groups and gender identity services that can assist them and the young people in their care (p 380).

Some foster carers can find it difficult to talk about LGBTQ+ issues because they are worried that they will use the wrong terminology

---

1 Lesbian, gay, bisexual, transgender, queer, and other orientations.

and cause offence. Supervising social workers can allay their fears by explaining that the terminology used is constantly evolving, and that as long as the carer is open to learning, asks for assistance and attempts to use the correct terms, people are unlikely to be offended. This will help to build the carer's confidence when it comes to discussing such issues with the child and others involved in their care.

The supervising social worker should also consider whether it would be appropriate for carers to create a gender-neutral environment within their household, regardless of whether they are currently caring for a young person who self-defines as LGBTQ+ or not. This could involve:

- using gender-neutral terms whenever possible (e.g. police officer rather than policeman, headteacher rather than headmaster/mistress);
- ensuring that toys and activities within the home are not defined by gender stereotypes;
- having a range of books, films, etc, in the home that celebrate diversity;
- always challenging discriminatory comments;
- being accepting and supportive of a young person experimenting with their appearance; and
- encouraging individuality.

If a foster carer is caring for a young person who is questioning their gender identity or defining themselves as LGBTQ+, the supervising social worker should encourage them to make it clear that they are available if the young person wishes to discuss their thoughts. However, these discussions should always take place at the young person's pace, and the carer should encourage them to self-identify and refrain from defining the young person's identity themselves. The worker should also ensure that the carer asks the young person what pronouns they would like the carer to use when speaking with and about them.

Where a young person has begun to address their gender or sexuality for the first time and discusses this information with the foster carer, the supervising social worker should ask the carer to encourage the young person to share their thinking with their own social worker, so that their needs can be addressed as part of their care plan. However, some young people may find this difficult, so the carer should make clear that this does not mean that they cannot still share their thoughts and feelings with the carer.

Supervising social workers can also help foster carers who are looking after LGBQT+ young people by providing them with details of organisations that can offer support and advice.

> **Further resources: LGBTQ+ young people**
>
> The following organisations provide a range of resources for young people and their foster carers on LGBT+ issues.
>
> LGBTQ+ Youth in Care – www.lgbtyouthincare.com
>
> The Proud Trust – www.theproudtrust.org
>
> Stonewall – www.stonewall.org.uk
>
> Action for Children – www.actionforchildren.org.uk
>
> New Family Social – https://newfamilysocial.org.uk
>
> Mermaids – https://mermaidsuk.org.uk

SUPPORTING FOSTER CARERS TO ADDRESS ISSUES OF DISCRIMINATION OR BULLYING

Young people in care can be susceptible to discrimination or bullying because they may be in a different living situation to others within their peer group. There can be an increased propensity for bullying if there are additional reasons why other children may view a young person as being different from them. A looked after child may be targeted because:

- they do not live with their birth family;
- English is not their first language;
- they abide by different cultural norms;
- they have gaps in their educational knowledge because of frequent moves;
- they do not have an established friendship group;
- they are LGBTQ+;
- they have a unique appearance;
- they lack some social skills because of their lived experience.

Therefore, it is important that foster carers can recognise such situations when they arise and know how to address them effectively. The supervising social worker can help by sharing some of the most common signs of bullying with foster carers, so that they can be alert to them. These can include the young person:

- not wanting to go to school;
- not wanting to go out into the local community;

- having unexplained cuts, bruises or other injuries;
- not having money, including school dinner money, but appearing very hungry when they return from school;
- frequently losing belongings;
- experiencing a loss of appetite;
- being unable to sleep;
- having inexplicable changes of mood;
- spending time alone and not wanting to associate with peers; and
- spending significant time on the internet and social media sites.

The supervising social worker should ensure that foster carers are alert to the potential for cyberbullying as well as in-person bullying, as this is a growing area of concern in relation to young people. It may be appropriate, at the point the young person joins the household, to confirm the household rules for the use of mobile phones and computers. For example, can they be used in bedrooms or after a certain time at night? Can the foster carer access the young person's devices to monitor what they are viewing? It is helpful if the fostering service itself has a clear policy on this. Bond (2021) provides useful introductory information on internet safety for fostering households.

The supervising social worker should also help each foster carer to find ways of addressing these issues with the young person and empowering the young person to build their self-esteem. The carer could, for example:

- enable the young person to establish a friendship group by inviting other young people to the foster home;
- help them to express and share their difficulties, and seek help from other safe adults, such as teaching staff;
- promote a household culture of open discussion and support, so that the young person feels able to express their fears.

> **Further resources: bullying and cyberbullying**
>
> Here are just a selection of the many websites that offer advice on bullying and cyberbullying.
>
> Bullying UK – www.bullying.co.uk
>
> NSPCC – www.nspcc.org.uk
>
> Young Minds – https://youngminds.org.uk
>
> UNICEF – www.unicef.org

> Anti-Bullying Alliance – www.anti-bullyingalliance.org.uk
>
> Act Against Bullying – https://actagainstbullying.org

Consideration also needs to be given to the fact that bullying can occur within, as well as outside of, the foster home. The supervising social worker should ensure that the issue of bullying is discussed in the household's safer caring policy, and that this is shared with all the household residents, so that everyone understands that this behaviour is not acceptable. This can also enable the worker to have an open discussion with the foster carer and other household members if bullying does occur.

Foster carers should be encouraged to role-model positive relationships by praising and rewarding acts of kindness performed by the young people in their care in order to develop positive household messages. They can also help looked after children by role-modelling non-discriminatory language, avoiding the use of stereotypes, and demonstrating how conflicts can be resolved through discussion, tolerance and acceptance.

Supervising social workers, in turn, can assist foster carers by role-modelling an inclusive approach that respects and values individuality, and promotes open discussions about equality and diversity. They should also ensure that their foster carers are aware of the fostering service's policies and procedures on equality, and that they have access to new materials as they become available so that they can increase their awareness of the issues involved.

Foster carers can also provide support to one another in these areas. These issues might be relatively new to some carers, so the supervising social worker could link a less experienced carer with another who can share their knowledge and personal accounts.

SUMMARY

Foster carers who are culturally competent, demonstrate self-awareness and who are committed to meeting the individual needs of each child can provide a positive experience of being looked after. However, there are times when the care offered to a child does not reach the required standard. In the next chapter, we consider the challenges that this presents for workers and how issues of concern should be addressed.

Chapter 10
Challenges for supervising social workers

Whilst supervising social workers have spoken in discussion groups about the positive aspects of working with foster carers, they have also highlighted some of the regular challenges they face when performing their role. This chapter examines some of the most common challenges and their potential solutions.

SAFEGUARDING MATTERS

The issue of safeguarding is of primary concern for everyone working in the childcare field, and it is important that foster carers understand their role in relation to this. NMS 4 emphasises that fostering services and foster carers need to protect children from abuse and neglect (DfE, 2011, p 14).

As mentioned in Chapter 5, the need to report any safeguarding concerns should be emphasised to foster carers as part of their induction training. The supervising social worker should continue to do this throughout their working relationship with the carers.

Foster carers need to understand that if they have any suspicions about a safeguarding issue, be it a bruise on a child following contact or a statement from a child that could be a disclosure, they need to inform their supervising social worker and the child's social worker as soon as possible. They should do this both verbally and in writing, and any contemporaneous record that they make should include the dates and times of observations and conversations.

Foster carers are usually provided with this information throughout their assessment and training. However, there may still be occasions when they do not understand their reporting obligations, or are uncertain about what they have seen or heard and are, therefore, reluctant to raise the issue in case they are mistaken. For instance, a foster carer may regularly take a child to contact and feel that they have developed a good rapport with the child's birth parent. They notice a bruise on the child post-contact, but both the child and birth parent seem calm and relaxed. As a result, they do not raise the issue with their supervising social worker because they are concerned about making a mistake and damaging their relationships with the child and with the parent. If, subsequently, the child discloses that an incident occurred during contact, the carer would not only be upset at their own decision-making but would also be asked to explain why they had not reported or recorded the concern.

This underlines the necessity for the supervising social worker to discuss regularly with their carers the need to safeguard children and to report any concerns in a timely manner. They should also be alert in supervision sessions for any indication that a carer is uneasy about a situation but seems hesitant to raise an issue. It is important to remember that this does not only apply to new foster carers, but can also apply to very experienced carers, who may have relaxed their approach to fostering over time.

However, not all safeguarding incidents occur outside the foster home, and so the next section focuses on concerns within foster homes.

Allegations, standards of care concerns, and complaints

During discussions between supervising social workers and the author, it emerged that one of the aspects of the role that creates the most tension between workers and carers, and which can therefore be a source of stress, is managing allegations, concerns and complaints. Unfortunately, this is something that workers will likely have to deal with on occasion. In fact, Lawson and Cann (2019) surveyed foster carers and found that one-third of them experienced an allegation of abuse or neglect during their fostering career (p 31). Williams' guide to managing allegations, concerns and complaints provides more detail about these processes (2021).

Fostering services appear to take differing approaches when addressing these issues. For example, in some services, supervising social workers undertake any investigations relating to concerns or allegations, while in others this work is undertaken by a social worker who is not known to the carers, or by an independent social worker. Some services permit their supervising social workers to continue to support carers during investigations, while others do not allow any supervising social worker who has been involved in the strategy meetings for an investigation to have contact with the carers during that investigation. Some services provide the carers with a different supervising social worker to support them during the process, while some provide support from an independent provider, such as the Fostering Network, or FosterTalk (which has a Fostering Independent Support Service (FISS)). Other fostering services offer both forms of support. Both FosterTalk and the

Fostering Network operate legal advice lines for members, as does CoramBAAF.

Plumridge and Sebba (2016) found that some supervising social workers were told that they 'could not discuss the allegation with the carer but could offer emotional support and advice and updates about procedures' (p 39). However, in other situations, foster carers were told that they were not allowed any further contact with their supervising social worker (p 39). Plumbridge and Sebba also found that foster carers under investigation often felt anger towards the fostering service, and that this was exacerbated by a lack of communication and information (pp 26–27). Thus, supervising social workers may find themselves on the receiving end of a carer's anger and frustration about the process and the system, particularly when the carer hears about the concerns for the first time.

Supervising social workers can find it difficult when discussing allegations or concerns with foster carers. They may find that the carer transfers their emotions about the situation onto them, and that they experience the strength of the carer's distress. The worker may also feel the need to defend themselves and the role that they played in any decision to hold an investigation. The key here is to remember that most people in this situation would respond emotionally. This may be the first time that the foster carer has been cognisant of any concerns. Additionally, they may not, at this early stage, be fully appraised of the details and may be keen to gather more information. It is also natural to try to defend oneself when criticised and to vent any feelings to the person providing the information.

The supervising social worker should find it easier to work with the foster carer and handle their own emotional responses if they:

- realise that a negative response from a carer is a natural defence mechanism;
- accept that any anger shown by the carer is directed at the system, not at them;
- provide the carer with clear messages about what can and cannot be shared with them at each stage of the process: and
- use their own supervision sessions to reflect on the process and its impact on themselves.

The supervising social worker's role and responsibilities

The supervising social worker should be fully conversant with their fostering service's policies and procedures, so that they can clearly convey information about the process to the foster carer. Each service should have a written policy about allegations, concerns and complaints in place that details the processes to be followed for each type of investigation. Supervising social workers should ensure that their foster carers receive details of this policy as part of their induction and understand it, as well as ensuring that they undertake training about the subject early in their fostering career. When an allegation or complaint is made, a carer may respond emotionally. This may mean that they are not able to fully comprehend any policies and processes that are explained to them at the time. If they are already familiar with these, they should be able to make more sense of the situation.

While explaining the service's policies and processes to the carers, the worker should ensure that they understand the difference between allegations, concerns and complaints.

NMS 22 spells out the fostering service's duties to handle:

> ...allegations and suspicions of harm...in a way that provides effective protection and support for children, the person making the allegation, and at the same time supports the person who is the subject of the allegation.

(DfE, 2011, p 44)

NMS 22.10 requires the fostering service to:

> ...ensure that a clear distinction is made between investigation into allegations of harm and discussions over standards of care. Investigations which find no evidence of harm should not become procedures looking into poor standards of care- these should be treated separately.

(DfE, 2011, p 45)

An **allegation** is information or suspicion that a person may have:

a. *behaved in a way that has, or may have, harmed a child;*

b. *possibly committed a criminal offence against or related to a child; or*

c. *behaved towards a child in a way that indicates he or she is unsuitable to work with children.*

(NMS 22.1, DfE, 2011, p 44)

A **standards of care concern** is an issue raised by the child in placement, their relatives or friends, or other professionals involved with the child or young person. Occasionally, they may be raised by members of the public. These are situations where the threshold for a safeguarding investigation has not been met but there are significant concerns about the quality of care being given. For example, there may be concerns about the physical household standards, or that a child's emotional, social or educational needs are not being met.

If the criteria for a section 47 investigation of an allegation or a standards of care investigation by the fostering service are not met, there may still be issues that should be addressed with the foster carer during supervision, and any discussion should be clearly marked on the foster carer's file and chronology.

A **complaint** is an issue raised by a child or young person in placement, relatives or friends, or professionals. This is dealt with under the fostering agency complaints process.

The pathways to exploring allegations, standards of care concerns and complaints are shown in Table 1.

Table 1: Allegations, concerns and complaints

1. Allegation			
Definition	**Process for exploration**	**Professionals' involvement**	**Actions necessary**
According to the Fostering Network's website, an 'allegation is an assertion from any person that a foster carer or another member of the fostering household has or may have behaved in a way that has harmed a child, committed a criminal offence against a child or behaved towards a child in a way that indicates they are unsuitable to work with children'	• Referral to Local Authority Designated Officer (LADO) • Strategy meeting • Investigation by someone independent of the foster carer, and other professionals, e.g. police, where necessary • Child usually interviewed early on as a priority	• Supervising social worker • Senior managers (LADO) • Police and other key professionals, as necessary	• Investigation, either via strategy and child protection policies or as single service (fostering). • Outcome to be considered by the fostering panel, and recorded in the foster carer's file and chronology

2. Standards of care concern			
Definition	**Process for exploration**	**Professionals' involvement**	**Actions necessary**
An issue raised about the care being provided to a child	• An initial professionals' meeting may be arranged	• Supervising social worker and their manager	• Action plan to address any issues raised
	• Discussion with the person raising the concerns, and with the foster carer and family	• Independent Review Officer (IRO) for reviews	• Issues to be considered on supervision visits and at the carer's annual reviews until resolved
	• Child usually interviewed early on as a priority	• Other key professionals as necessary	• Record of issues to be added to the carer's file and chronology
			• If there are significant causes for concern, a detailed investigation may be needed. A senior fostering manager should decide whether the carer should be presented to the panel for consideration of their approval

3. Complaint			
Definition	**Process for exploration**	**Professionals' involvement**	**Actions necessary**
A complaint made about the care provided to a child using the service's formal complaints process	Terms of reference to be drawn up and an investigation undertaken in line with the service's complaints process	Complaints investigation with an investigator who has no connection to the foster carer	Investigation report to be reviewed by a senior manager, and outcomes to be recorded in the carer's file and chronology. Return to panel if required

The supervising social worker should be clear about their role in an investigation and have discussed this with their own supervisor. For example, will they:

- continue to supervise the carer during an investigation?
- offer the carer support in relation to the investigation or arrange for them to have independent support?
- undertake the investigation? or
- cease contact with the carer during the investigation?

One of the key dilemmas for a supervising social worker is the conflict they experience in ensuring that they provide a robust, objective assessment of the situation whilst providing support to potentially very distressed foster carers, whether they are undertaking the investigation or even just contributing to meetings and discussions about it. In order to assist with this dilemma, the worker should advocate on the carer's behalf to ensure that:

- appropriate support is available to them;
- there will be ongoing support for them throughout the process;
- they have received as much written information about their position as possible; and
- they have been informed of their rights.

The role of the supervising social worker is to ensure that either they or, if they cannot fulfil the role, another person provides the correct level of support to the foster carer. The emotional impact of an allegation on a carer can be immense. Being the subject of an allegation can also be isolating, as carers are often told that they cannot discuss the allegation with anyone but their supporting worker, and this may mean that their usual sources of support, such as family members, members of fostering support groups, or buddy carers, are not available to them.

If the supervising social worker continues to support the fostering household, it can impact their working relationship. The worker may not be able to provide the carer with the information they want, for example, or the carer may consider the worker to be aligned with the investigation and therefore "not on their side". In such cases, the worker may lose the carer's trust.

Sometimes, this situation can be avoided if the supervising social worker has a clear conversation with the foster carer at the beginning of the investigation. During this discussion, they should explain:

- their role in the investigation;
- what information they will and will not be able to provide to the carer;
- the support that they can offer to the carer;
- the statutory requirements of the supervising social worker's role if the carer is continuing to care for children during an investigation;
- the carer's legal and procedural rights in the situation; and
- where the carer can go for additional support.

Ideally, this information should be provided both verbally and in writing to minimise the chances that the carer will become confused or fail to understand it, as they may be in a distressed state.

The emotional impact on the supervising social worker

The fostering service also needs to acknowledge the impact that supporting foster carers in these situations can have on supervising social workers and other workers involved. They should ensure that these workers have the opportunity to discuss how absorbing carers' emotional responses is affecting them and offer them appropriate support.

Supervising social workers can experience a range of complex emotions and thoughts during an investigation. They are employed by the service that has triggered an investigation and, as registered social workers, they have a duty to safeguard children. However, they may also find it difficult to discover that a carer with whom they have a close working relationship, and whom they feel they know well, has been accused of inappropriate actions or behaviour.

Their instinctive reaction may be to defend the foster carer and negate the allegations in order to rationalise their experience of them. This is a normal response and should not be seen as an indication that their relationship with the carer does not have appropriate boundaries. By seeking support from a manager or supervisor, the supervising social worker may be able to see the situation from a more objective point of view, and this could make it easier for them and the carer to work through the situation.

Discussing issues with foster carers

The supervising social worker may be allocated the task of sharing the allegations, concerns or complaints with the carer. This can be a positive choice for the carer, as the worker will know them, have an idea of their potential responses, and be able to shape a conversation in a supportive way. However, it can be helpful if the supervising social worker is accompanied by their manager, so that they can provide the carer with details of the formal process that will take place. This has the trifold purpose of making it clear that it is the fostering service that has the concern and not the individual staff member, ensuring that there is a witness to the conversation, and providing support for the supervising social worker. The information conveyed to the foster carer during this discussion should also be provided to them in writing.

When allegations or complaints have been made, the terms of reference for the investigation impose structure on the initial discussions with foster carers. However, a supervising social worker may find it more challenging to raise concerns about standards of care during a supervision session, and the following advice on how to prepare for such a conversation may be useful.

> **Preparing for a challenging conversation**
>
> - *What is the issue that needs addressing?*
> - *Is there more than one issue?*
> - *Why is the issue important?*
> - *Why is it challenging for me to address this issue with this person?*
> - *What are my feelings about this issue?*
> - *What are my feelings about the person concerned?*
> - *What are my feelings about me and my role in this situation?*
> - *How might those feelings affect the conversation?*
> - *Can I articulate the issue?*
> - *Do I have examples of behaviour or events which illustrate the issue?*
> - *What is the message I wish to communicate?*
> - *What is the outcome I am seeking from this conversation?*
> - *What is my motivation for having this conversation?*
>
> (Beddoe and Davys, 2016, p 197)

However, while planning a conversation can help a supervising social worker to convey their concerns, the worker cannot predict the foster carer's response and, as the carer may be shocked, dismayed or distressed, they may find it difficult to formulate responses in the first instance.

The supervising social worker could inform the foster carer that they wish to discuss an allegation or concern with them during their next visit. However, one carer noted, in discussion with the author, that they were told there was a concern on a Friday, with a visit planned for Monday morning, and spent all weekend wondering what the issue was and worrying about it. They stated that they would have preferred not to have been told about the discussion in advance. The supervising social worker should therefore base their decision about how to raise concerns on their knowledge of the carer and their potential reaction.

It is also worth remembering that when discussing concerns with people, they tend to hear and focus on parts of the information being provided, particularly any negative sections, rather than the conversation as a whole. Therefore, there is an argument for providing the information, repeating it in sections, and asking the carer for their comments, to ensure that they have absorbed everything.

Record-keeping in relation to allegations and standard of care concerns

Supervising social workers should record any discussions that take place about fostering practice concerns in a supervision record or, if necessary, a separate document. The record should include full details of the concerns, the foster carer's views, an agreed plan of action, and information about how progress to address the issues will be measured. The worker should also refer to this in the carer's next annual review and record it on a chronology, so that patterns of concerns can be identified.

The *Children Act Guidance and Regulations Fostering Services: Volume 4* (HM Government, 2011, pp 26–27) clearly details the retention period for allegations to foster carers:

> *In accordance with Working Together, it is important to keep on the foster carer's record a clear and comprehensive summary of any allegations made, details of how the allegation was followed up and resolved, and details of any action taken and decisions reached, and to make this available to the individual. Notwithstanding the requirements of regulation 32 regarding retention of records, such information should be retained on file at least until the person concerned reaches normal retirement age, or for 10 years if that is longer. The purpose of the record is to enable accurate information to be given in response to any future request for a reference.*

Outcomes of investigations

While these may vary from service to service, there is generally consensus that investigations can have one of five possible outcomes. The allegation or concern can be deemed to be:

- Substantiated – there is evidence to support the allegation or concern.

- False – there is evidence to disprove the allegation or concern.

- Malicious – the information was false and there was an intention to deceive.

- Unfounded – there is no evidence to support the allegation or concern, and there are indications that the person raising the issue may have been mistaken about what they saw or heard or did not have full information.

- Unsubstantiated – there is insufficient evidence to support or refute the allegation. This is not the same as a finding of false, and therefore is a neutral outcome that does not imply guilt or innocence.

Hearing that an allegation against them is substantiated can be devastating for foster carers. However, in many ways, the last finding of unsubstantiated is also difficult for carers as it can feel like they have been left in limbo, without "clearing their name". In discussions with the author, foster carers have said that it feels like the allegation or concern will always be a shadow over their fostering career. Therefore, supervising social workers should try to help carers to understand the neutrality of such an outcome and to look for the positives in the situation.

The post-investigation process

Where an allegation has been made and a strategy meeting has resulted in a formal investigation, the outcome of the investigation and an updated review of the foster carer should be presented to the fostering panel so that they can consider whether the carer continues to meet the NMS for fostering. If significant safeguarding concerns are substantiated, these will be reported to the DBS and Ofsted will be notified.

Where a standard of care concern has been resolved and any agreed actions achieved, this issue should be regarded as concluded and only referred to in future if a pattern of concerns emerges. If the concerns have not been resolved, the supervising social worker and their manager should consider whether the issue should be raised at the fostering panel. If so, they should arrange for a review of the foster carer to take place. This should be presented to the panel so that they have a holistic view of the carer. If the panel recommends changes to the foster carer's approval or deregistration and the carer does not agree with this, they have the right, within 28 working days, to ask the fostering decision-maker to review this decision, or to apply to the Independent Review Mechanism (IRM) in England or Wales for a review of their case.

In the above scenarios, it is the supervising social worker's role to ensure that all relevant information is presented to the fostering panel. They should also make sure that the foster carer understands the process, and is supported to attend the panel and express their views. It may be appropriate for the supervising social worker to support the carer, but if they have been part of the investigation and their relationship with the carer is strained, they should advocate appropriate support for the carer instead.

Dealing with allegations and standards of care concerns is a complex and challenging area of work for supervising social workers. Emotions often run high in terms of their concerns for children in placement and the foster carers, and the implications for all parties in the future. The supervising social worker may have many conflicting thoughts and feelings until the relevant information has been gathered. It is important for the worker to be able to access high-quality supervision at these times, to understand the role of the LADO, and to be able to contact them for advice.

Complaints investigations

Complaints about foster carers are rarer than allegations or standards of care concerns, but where a foster carer has been the subject of a formal complaint, the supervising social worker's role is to support them whilst an independent person completes the investigation. On receipt of the completed enquiry, the manager commissioning the investigation should share the outcome, together with their decisions about any actions to be taken in relation to the complaint, with the supervising social worker and their manager. This may include creating a development plan for the carer or, when significant issues have been found, preparing the carer for a return to the fostering panel.

Investigated complaints should be referred to in the foster carer's next annual review. They should not be referred to in ongoing reviews unless a new, similar complaint arises, but a record should always be maintained on the chronology in the carer's file. If a serious complaint has been substantiated and a return to the fostering panel is required, a review of the carer should be held, with the supervising social worker writing the report and presenting it at the panel, and including full details of the complaint and its outcome. It can be helpful in these situations if the writer of the complaint enquiry attends the fostering panel to respond to any issues raised about it. This will enable the worker to support the carer.

Working relationships after an allegation, concern or complaint

If a foster carer is continuing to work for the service following the resolution of an allegation, concern or complaint, the supervising social worker should consider their relationship with them. If they have had challenging conversations with the carer, they may need to undertake reparative work in order to re-establish a strong working relationship. Although a change of supervising social worker may be needed in some cases so that the care being provided to children is not negatively impacted, many relationships can be repaired through mediation. This should be facilitated by a manager or an IRO so that the carer can express their feelings and know that these have been acknowledged, and the worker can explain their role and the service's requirements in these situations. Ideally, this will end with all parties agreeing to move forward with a refreshed working relationship.

Foster carers should be encouraged to repair a working relationship with their supervising social worker if possible. Doing so could help the carer to think about how they could repair a relationship with a child or young person they are caring for, for example, after an event has taken place that impacts on trust.

RESISTANT CARERS

Some foster carers may seem reluctant to meet all or some of the fostering requirements and regulations, despite providing the children placed with them with high-quality care. They may, for example, refuse to keep regular diary recordings, to attend training, to make themselves available for supervision sessions, or to address particular health and safety issues. This may be because they feel that undertaking a required action will not make a difference in practical terms, or believe that the supervising social worker has overly high expectations.

The supervising social worker should address these issues before they become entrenched. Ideally, all of the requirements of the fostering task should have been spelt out to the carer during their initial training and induction, in the fostering handbook, and in the contract drawn up between each carer and their fostering service. The worker can, therefore, refer to these resources when talking to the carer. However, they should also remind the carer that the fostering approval relates to the whole household and not just to the primary carer. Therefore, all foster carers in the household must complete the mandatory training and participate in supervision sessions.

When addressing such "stuck" issues, the supervising social worker could use the challenging conversations preparation questions featured earlier in this chapter, with an additional question: 'Where is this laid out in the fostering service requirements or national standards?' This can show the carer that the requirement being made of them applies to all foster carers.

If a supervising social worker states that foster carers *must* comply with requirements, a power struggle can develop. This can lead to the worker and the carer becoming polarised, making the situation more difficult to resolve. The worker could approach this more productively by presenting the situation to the carer as a shared problem – they could explain to the carer that the service requires all of its carers to attend certain training courses, that this has not been happening in this case, and that they would like the carer to work with them to find a solution to the problem.

The supervising social worker should also investigate whether the carer has a reason for noncompliance that they are unable to articulate. For example:

- Is the carer failing to keep records because they have undisclosed literacy problems?

- Is the carer reluctant to attend face-to-face training sessions because they dislike talking in groups?

- Does the carer have financial issues that mean they are unable to address health and safety issues or attend training?

- Where there are two carers, is one opting out of involvement due to relationship issues?

Although the supervising social worker needs to make the service's expectations clear, it is crucial for them to encourage the carer to share details of anything that is preventing them from meeting the fostering regulations and, where possible, to provide them with support and solutions.

FLEXIBILITY WITH FAMILY AND FRIENDS CARERS

It is also important for the supervising social worker to give additional consideration to the expectations of family and friends carers. Section 5.19 of the *Family and Friends Care: Statutory guidance for local authorities* (DfE, 2010) states that 'a different approach may be needed to assessing family and friends foster carer compared to other foster carer applications' (p 35), highlighting that they are assessed to look after a specific child, such as a grandchild, and are not seeking to be professional foster carers. It also suggests that there should be a degree of flexibility with regard to some key issues, such as bedroom sharing (s.5.30, p 37), health issues (s.5.35, p 39), and past criminal convictions (s.5.38, p 39). Where this is the case, it is important that the decisions are clearly evidenced.

It therefore follows that services could be flexible with family and friends carers with regard to absolute adherence to fostering standards.

> **GOOD PRACTICE EXAMPLE**
>
> A fostering panel heard a first review of a grandfather who was doing a superb job of caring for his granddaughter. He was liaising with school, supporting family contact, and providing a high level of care. However, he was not engaging with the TSD standards work or any of the required training. The panel therefore reminded him of the requirements, whilst praising his care of the young person, and asked him to attend training as soon as possible.
>
> One year later, following the annual review, the IRO asked for the case to be referred to the fostering panel as the carer had still not completed his TSD standards workbook or attended any training sessions. The panel knew that the service was considering whether to recommend the deregistration of the carer or encourage him to apply for a special guardianship order, as this might fit his situation better. However, the carer valued the support that he was receiving from the fostering service and wished to continue working for them.
>
> Eventually, the service and the carer negotiated a solution, with the full support of the fostering panel. They agreed that he would complete his TSD standards with help from his supervising social worker during additional supervision sessions, and that he would attend the first aid training. The rest of the mandatory training would be delivered to him by the supervising social worker on a one-to-one basis, as he respected her knowledge and ability to explain issues to him in a way that he understood and found relevant to his situation.
>
> Had this flexible solution not been found, the carer may have been deregistered for noncompliance with the regulations, possibly resulting in his granddaughter losing her placement with a grandparent who loved and cared for her.

It may also be possible to be more flexible with family and friends carers in relation to recordings, either by asking them to provide these less frequently, allowing them to use voice-activated computer software, or arranging for carers who lack IT skills to dictate their recordings to staff members over the phone.

FLEXIBLE SOLUTIONS FOR MAINSTREAM CARERS

While it may not be feasible for fostering services to be as flexible about fostering requirements and regulations with mainstream foster carers, who are caring for a range of children (including children of different ages, those who are staying for varying amounts of time, and those whose history they do not know), the supervising social worker may still be able to find innovative ways to resolve failures to comply without causing the carers to disengage.

For example, many fostering services now require carers to attend a set number of support groups each year. However, in some households where there are two foster carers, the primary carer will attend the sessions but the secondary carer will fail to do so. The supervising social workers in one service, where the majority of the secondary carers were male and in full-time employment, opted to hold support groups for male (primary and secondary) carers on a Saturday morning at a venue that provided breakfasts and attendance improved dramatically.

Whenever the supervising social worker needs to discuss complex issues of non-compliance with regulations and policies with a foster carer, they should keep a record of the conversation, which should be shared with the foster carer and, if appropriate, referred to in the carer's annual review. They should also record the issues and discussions in the carer's chronology.

COMPASSION FATIGUE

In her foreword to Ottaway and Selwyn's *No-One Told us it was Going to be Like This: Compassion fatigue and foster carers*, Naish describes compassion fatigue as a 'lonely desperate place to be. It destroys confidence, relationships and even whole families' (2016, p 4).

Compassion fatigue is also known as "blocked care". When experiencing it, a foster carer can become incapable of empathising with and supporting the child because their mind and body are protecting them from the secondary trauma they are experiencing. The care that they offer becomes more reactive to problems, as they find it impossible to consider the individual child and their needs. The carer may also focus on the negatives about the child and their behaviour, and lose the ability to see any positives.

Ottaway and Selwyn (2016) refer to three dimensions of compassion fatigue, initially identified by Stamm in 2010:

- **Burnout** – those dealing with traumatised people can eventually feel exhausted (both physically and mentally), hopeless, frustrated or angry.

- **Secondary trauma stress** – develops when the individual becomes directly affected by the trauma experienced by those they are caring for and/or supporting at work.

- **Compassion satisfaction** – associated with the positive aspects of providing care to others in the working environment, and includes such features as altruism, satisfaction with the work undertaken with those affected by trauma, and the support derived from team members.

(Adapted from Ottoway and Selywn's (2016) summary of Stamm's (2010) work)

Stamm's theory was designed to reflect the experiences of professionals working with people who had experienced trauma as part of their working lives, many of whom had blocks of time when they were not at work that they could use to relax, and undertake hobbies and activities.

In many ways, it is unsurprising that some foster carers also suffer from compassion fatigue. All fostering services require their carers to work in a therapeutic way with children who have insecure attachments so that the child can recover from their trauma. Foster carers live with the child and their needs 24 hours a day, and this can place emotional and physical strain on them. Sometimes, the carers' own bodies and minds may intervene, and shut down to protect them from further exposure to trauma.

Assisting foster carers with compassion fatigue

Firstly, the supervising social worker can help the foster carer to identify their feelings and decide whether they are experiencing compassion fatigue. They may be able to do this in reflective conversation, but some carers may find it helpful to complete a questionnaire instead. Ideally, the training provided to the carer should have covered compassion fatigue, so that they understand what it is and can recognise the signs, such as sleep difficulties, anxiety, panic attacks, anger, irritability, feeling isolated, and being unable to respond with empathy to a child.

The Professional Quality of Life Scale (ProQOL) (see Appendix 2) is one tool that supervising social workers could encourage foster carers to use to help recognise their feelings. This document can be readily accessed online. An individual's answers to the questions are assessed according to the Compassion Satisfaction, Burnout and Secondary Traumatic Stress scales. The results show whether the individual has recorded a low, moderate or high score in each area, and what this may mean for them.

Secondly, the supervising social worker should try to help the foster carer understand that compassion fatigue is not an unusual response to this type of work. They should reassure the carer by informing them that they can recover and repair themselves so that they can continue to care for others. The carer can begin the process by engaging in self-care – ensuring that they eat well, adopt a good sleep pattern, take time out for activities that they enjoy, and accept that, at this moment, they need assistance from others.

This assistance may take the form of providing respite care for the child placed. Many foster carers are reluctant to agree to this, believing that it could cause further trauma to a child who may already feel rejected. Therefore, such a proposal will need to be handled sensitively and the supervising social worker will need to explain to the carer and child why they need a break from each other. It is also important to remember that respite care does not need to include overnight stays. Sometimes a fostering service can arrange for a child to participate in activities with a staff member or another foster carer during the day instead. Whatever the proposed solution, the worker should encourage the carer to consider their needs as well as those of the child, and help them to understand that they cannot help anyone else unless they feel healthy and mentally fit.

Ideally, any respite provided should be flexible and responsive, so that it can be used at moments of crisis and when the foster carer is feeling overwhelmed. However, the supervising social worker may also want to consider establishing a planned respite care programme. One option would be for the worker to help the carer to form a buddying partnership with another carer. If the child regularly spends the day with another foster family for play dates or outings, they can receive respite care on a flexible, normalised basis, without even being aware that their carer needs a break. This is where initiatives such as the Mockingbird Programme (referred to in Chapter 5) have benefits for the child, in that they stay for "sleepovers" with foster carers and children whom they already know well.

Some successful foster carers who take intensive assessment placements, such as parent and child placements, build set breaks into their schedules so that they can relax and recuperate between placements. This can help them to avoid burnout and compassion fatigue. Supervising social workers could also try to ensure that carers who take short-term placements are matched with children who are not known to have had significant trauma, shortly after looking after children who are affected by this. However, this is not always possible when there is a shortage of foster carers.

Some fostering services employ psychologists who are able to offer foster carers sessions so that they can focus on their needs, rather than on those of the children placed with them. This can give carers the time and space they need to understand their own reactions to fostering, and to consider how they can care for themselves and develop resilience.

> **Assisting foster carers to address compassion fatigue**
>
> A supervising social worker can:
>
> - help the carer to recognise the signs and symptoms of compassion fatigue;
>
> - enable the carer to recognise when they are experiencing this;
>
> - listen to the carer with empathy and be non-judgmental;
>
> - ensure that individual and group peer support is available to the carer;
>
> - encourage the carer to focus on self-care;
>
> - provide responsive and flexible respite care;
>
> - offer the carer access to psychological support;
>
> - offer the carer "recovery time" between placements;
>
> - try to vary the placements offered to the carer so that they are not constantly dealing with children with complex needs.

The supervising social worker should also reflect on their own reactions to foster carers who are experiencing compassion fatigue. For example, a carer whose compassion fatigue has not yet been recognised may appear to be lacking empathy or failing to understand a child and their behaviour. As a result, the worker may doubt whether the carer has the skills to meet the child's needs, and whether their expectations of the child are unrealistic. This may cause the worker to feel frustrated with the carer or overprotective of the child. While the worker may be able to ensure that the carer remains unaware of their reaction, they may still respond to the carer differently. Therefore, workers must be aware of the possibility of compassion fatigue at all times, ensure that they are always able to demonstrate empathy for their carers, and use their own supervision sessions to explore their responses to such situations.

ENDINGS AND DISRUPTIONS

An unplanned ending to a placement can occur for many reasons. A child who is the subject of an interim care order may be returned to their parents, for example, or a foster carer may become unwell or reach a crisis point where they no longer feel able to meet the child's needs. When a foster carer has not been able to prepare for a child moving on, they may well feel loss and may wish to discuss this with their supervising social worker. If the foster carer feels that the reunification plan was not in the child's interests, they may need a safe space in which to air these views.

However, when a permanent/long-term placement ends abruptly, it is considered to have been disrupted. In such cases, foster carers may experience a range of emotions. If the carer has been finding it difficult to manage a child's behaviour, they may feel some relief, but they may also feel guilty because the child has had to move again. If the child or young person has instigated the ending, the carer may feel anger, distress or concern, particularly if an allegation has been made against them.

Most fostering services have policies about the process that should be followed in such circumstances so that all parties can understand why the placement came to an end. Usually this requires a disruption meeting so that everyone involved can consider what has been learned from the placement's termination. Disruption meetings can also be useful when some short-term placements end, if significant lessons can be learned from them. However, before the foster carer can participate in the meeting, the supervising social worker will need to help them to:

- express their emotions and feelings;
- understand the contributory factors to the ending;
- assess whether the ending was foreseeable; and
- consider whether they can learn anything from the situation.

It may take several discussions for the foster carer to be able to share all of their emotions, as they may not initially be able to consider the situation in a detached way. This may be complicated for their supervising social worker, who may have their own emotional reaction to the situation. The worker may have known the young person for several years and feel the loss themselves. They may have had concerns about the carer's approach to the young person and feel frustrated that they could not bring about change. They may feel upset if they believe that the carer precipitated an unplanned ending that could have been avoided. It is therefore important for the supervising social worker to talk openly with their supervisor, release their feelings, and put these in perspective before they try to help the carer to address the disruption.

Foster carers can often be reluctant to attend disruption meetings and will need support and advice to enable them to participate fully. When talking to the foster carer, the supervising social worker should stress that the meeting is not about apportioning blame for the disruption, but about learning from the experience in order to prevent future disruptions. These meetings can also help to ensure that all parties are united in their attempts to provide the best placements possible for children.

The supervising social worker can help the foster carer to prepare for the meeting by creating a timeline of significant events (including positive ones) that occurred during the placement, which they can refer to later. They should also provide the carer with a clear explanation of who will be present at the meeting and the agenda, and reassure them that they can take a break from it at any time.

Even where endings are planned, the emotional impact on foster carers can be immense. In their journal paper, 'Disenfranchised grief: the emotional impact experienced by foster carers on the cessation of a placement', Lynes and Sitoe (2019, p 27) noted that:

> *People, including social workers, rarely understood the intensity of the carers' grief and that this was reflected in the level and type of support they received. They said they were expected to behave in an emotionally detached manner...Many participants thought that their grief was not recognised as legitimate by others and felt the need to conceal it for fear of being deemed unprofessional.*

This echoes the findings of Boswell and Cudmore (2014), who researched planned moves for children from foster care to adoptive homes. They noted that as introductory plans progressed, foster carers moved to using language about the child that was less emotional and more about doing a professional job. When talking about the period prior to the move, 'it was clear that foster carers were processing some very painful feelings and many were explicit about how giving into these feelings was incompatible with retaining a professional stance' (p 10). The social workers that they interviewed also 'spoke about the need for the foster carer to remain "professional" and not let her emotions spill out publicly, to protect the adoptive parent from being burdened with the child's attachment and impending loss' (p 10).

Feelings of grief are not confined to planned endings. Hebert *et al* (2013) found that 'carers may also feel grief when they request a child be removed or have had insufficient time to prepare for the departure' (p 255).

This means that foster carers may be trying to contain feelings of loss and need support to express these emotions freely, without feeling that they are not acting in a professional manner.

The role for the supervising social worker when a foster carer is coming to terms with the loss of a child is to:

- acknowledge and accept the carer's sense of loss and grief;

- enable all members of the household to express their emotions freely;

- provide additional visits and phone contact immediately after the child's move;

- offer the carer support from a buddy carer;

- enable the carer to discuss the child and their time in the fostering household;
- assist the carer in thinking about their household without this child in residence, if the move is planned;
- plan moves and ensure there are opportunities for good partings whenever possible;
- ensure that, if ongoing contact with the child is possible and in the child's interests, this is planned and occurs;
- make sure that, where ongoing contact is not possible, the carer understands why;
- provide updates about the child's well-being and progress to the carer, where practicable;
- acknowledge the key role that the carer has played in this child's life;
- facilitate discussions at support groups about grief and loss when children move on.

The key to dealing with all of these issues is for the supervising social worker to keep in mind that everyone involved in supporting a child in placement will experience emotional responses to situations that arise in caring for that child. The worker must therefore acknowledge and address their own emotions and then support the carer so that they can do the same.

Chapter 11
Conclusion

This practice guide has considered the role of the supervising social worker in depth. It has considered the history of the development of the job, from its origins in the role of the children's officers responsible for child welfare to the complex social work role that it is today. The original role focused on household conditions rather than on the skills and abilities of foster carers, and the assessment of carers' abilities was only given sharper focus with the introduction of the Children Act 1989 and subsequent fostering regulations. These required a more detailed assessment of foster carers, and emphasised the need for the provision of training, advice and support.

It has also shown how academic research and the outcomes of case reviews reveal that, whilst foster carers highly value the support they receive from supervising social workers, this support needs to include an element of critical appraisal and challenge, together with a recognition of any patterns of concern, and for those concerns to be addressed in a timely and robust manner.

The main tasks undertaken by supervising social workers and the challenges that they face while working with foster carers have been examined in detail. As a result, a number of key points have been identified.

- In order to develop a professional working relationship with foster carers, the supervising social worker must create partnerships with all members of the fostering household. This will ensure that every family member feels able to raise any issues they have in relation to the fostering task.

- The supervising social worker should also establish the structure of the supervision through the use of a written agreement with the foster carer, and consider using a supervision model to ensure consistency. It is also helpful if the worker understands their carer's learning style and uses this knowledge to shape the learning opportunities available to them, as this will enable the carer to develop their skills and expertise. Foster carers should also be encouraged to be reflective, and to work in an inclusive and anti-discriminatory way. The supervising social worker can use a coaching approach to support this, whilst ensuring that they always retain an element of professional curiosity.

- Where foster carers appear to be resistant to the support on offer, the supervising social worker should consider all potential reasons for this, including the possibility of compassion fatigue. Skilled support may be needed in order for the parties involved to be able to overcome these blocks.

- If foster carers are subject to allegations or complaints, the supervising social worker's role is first and foremost to safeguard children, to undertake a robust evidence-based assessment if required, and to enable the carers to understand the issues and provide support. However, if it is not possible for them to undertake this themselves, they need to ensure that each carer is supported and that whoever provides that support is aware of their individual needs.

- It is important to note that supervising social workers need to possess a range of skills in order to be able to perform the role effectively, including in-depth knowledge of childcare, child development and attachment theory; an understanding of the impact of trauma and loss; the ability to work as part of a team with other professionals; and diplomacy skills. They can also become emotionally drained by some of the issues that they deal with, so it is important for them to have excellent reflective supervision.

The primary aim behind all of this good practice is to endeavour to safeguard children in care, to ensure that they receive high-quality, individual care and that they are given the opportunity to develop to their full potential. The supervising social worker role is a key component in the care of looked after children, and those performing it manage to be supporters, teachers, inspectors, assessors, coaches, mediators, networkers, colleagues, and counsellors. However, it is also a constantly evolving role, and the limited amount of research that has been carried out in respect of the role and lack of specialist training available implies that its complexity and value are not always acknowledged. Hopefully, this guide goes some way towards demonstrating just how critical the role is and will help those performing it to be able to acquire the tools they need in order to excel.

References

Adams P (2019a) *Undertaking Checks and References in Fostering and Adoption Assessments* (2nd edn), London: CoramBAAF

Adams P (2019b) *Undertaking a Foster Carer Review* (2nd ed), London: CoramBAAF

Adams P (2021) *Devising and Updating Risk Assessment and Management Plans in Fostering*, London: CoramBAAF

Adams P and Dibben E (2020) *Parent and Child Fostering* (2nd ed), London: CoramBAAF

Adams P and Jordan L (2019) *Complying with the GPR and DPA 2018*, London: CoramBAAF

Beddoe L and Davys A (2016) *Challenges in Professional Supervision: Current themes and models for practice*, London: Jessica Kingsley Publishers

Bentley-Lawson N (2017) *Serious Case Review: Child T*, Warwick: Warwickshire Safeguarding Children Board

Bond H (2021) *Things Foster Carers Need to Know: Young people and internet safety*, London: CoramBAAF

Boswell S and Cudmore L (2014) '"The children were fine": acknowledging complex feelings in the move from foster care into adoption', *Adoption & Fostering*, 38:1, pp 5–21

Brighton and Hove City Council (undated) *Me and My World Review: A guide for carers and professionals*, available at www.brighton-hove.gov.uk/me-and-my-world-review-guide-carers-and-professionals

Brighton and Hove Local Safeguarding Children Board (2017) *Working Together to Improve Professional Curiosity*, Brighton: Brighton and Hove LSCB

Bunday L, Dallos R, Morgan K and McKenzie R (2015) 'Foster carers' reflective understanding of parenting looked after children: an exploratory study', *Adoption & Fostering*, 39:2, pp 145–158

Butler J (2009) *Behaviour*, London: Fostering Network

Care of Children Committee (1946) *Report of the Care of Children Committee*, London: HMSO

Children's Partnership (2014) *Staying Put: Good practice guide*, London: Children's Partnership

Cleaver H and Rose W (2020) *Safeguarding Children living with Foster Carers, Adopters and Special Guardians: Learning from serious case reviews 2007–2019*, London: CoramBAAF

Clyde J (1946) *The Clyde Report on Homeless Children*, Edinburgh: HMSO

Coates P (2013) *Goal Setting Workshop*, available at: https://slideplayer.com/slide/4602977/

Cosis Brown H (2015) *Foster Carer Reviews: Process, practicalities and best practice*, London: CoramBAAF

Cosis Brown H, Sebba J and Luke N (2014) *The Role of the Supervising Social Worker in Foster Care: An international literature review*, Oxford: Rees Centre

Cross TL, Bazron B, Dennis K and Isaacs M (1989) *Towards a Culturally Competent System of Care: A monograph on effective services for minority children who are severely emotionally disturbed*, Washington DC: CASSP Technical Assistance Center

Department for Education (2010) *Family and Friends Care: Statutory guidance for local authorities*, London: DfE

Department for Education (2011) *Fostering Services: National minimum standards for fostering*, London: DfE

Department for Education (2012) *Training, Support and Development Standards for Foster Care: Guidance for managers, supervising social workers*, London: DfE

Department of Child Protection (2011) *The Signs of Safety: Child protection practice framework* (2nd ed), East Perth: Government of Western Australia

Elliott A (2013) *Why Can't My Child Behave? Empathetic parenting strategies that work for adoptive and foster families*, London: Jessica Kingsley Publishers

Fleming ND and Mills C (1992) 'Not another inventory, rather a catalyst for reflection', *To Improve the Academy*, 11, pp 137–149

Fostering Network (2015) *Head, Heart, Hands: Introducing social pedagogy in foster care*, London: Fostering Network, available from https://www.thefosteringnetwork.org.uk/sites/www.fostering.net/files/content/head_heart_hands_impact_report.pdf

Fostering Network (2016a) *Advice and Information Page*, available at: https://www.thefosteringnetwork.org.uk/advice-information

Fostering Network (2016b) *Social Pedagogy in Practice: Building resilience*, available at: https://www.thefosteringnetwork.org.uk/policy-practice/head-heart-hands/social-pedagogy-in-practice

Fursland E (2017) *Caring for a Child who has been Sexually Exploited*, London: CoramBAAF

Gardner H (1983) *Frames of Mind*, New York: Basic Books

Geiger J, Piel MH and Leitz C (2013) 'Should I stay or should I go? A mixed methods study examining the factors influencing foster parents' decisions to continue or discontinue providing foster care', *Children and Youth Services Review*, 35:9, pp 1356–1365

Greenaway R (1992) 'Reviewing by doing', *Journal of Adventure, Education and Outdoor Leadership*, available at: https://reviewing.co.uk/articles/2rbd.htm

Hawkins S and Unnamed Local Safeguarding Children Board (2019) *Serious Case Review No. 2019/C7931: Managed review of Child F*, London: NSPCC on behalf of an unnamed local safeguarding children board

Hebert C, Kulkin HS and McLean M (2013) 'Grief and foster parents: how do foster parents feel when a foster child leaves their home?', *Adoption & Fostering*, 37:3, pp 253–267

HM Government (2011, updated 2015) *The Children Act 1989 Guidance and Regulations Volume 4: Fostering services*, London: HM Government

Höjer I, Sebba J and Luke N (2013) *The Impact of Fostering on Foster Carers' Children: An international literature review*, Oxford: Rees Centre

Home Office (1945) *Report by Sir William Monckton KCMG KCVO MC KC: On the circumstances which led to the boarding out of Dennis and Terence O'Neill at Bank Farm, Minsterly and the steps taken to supervise their welfare, etc*, London: Home Office

Honey P and Mumford A (2016) *Learning Styles Questionnaire*, available at: https://www.talentlens.com/uk/career-development/honey-and-mumford-learning-styles-questionnaire.html

Hughes DA (2006) *Building the Bonds of Attachment: Awakening love in deeply troubled children*, Northvale, NJ: Jason Aronson

Hughes DA (2009) *Attachment-Focused Parenting: Effective strategies to care for children*, New York: WW Norton & Company

Ibbetson K (2014) *Serious Case Review, Overview Report: The sexual abuse of children in a foster home*, London: City and Hackney Safeguarding Children Board

Jagger C (2018) 'The supervising social worker in an inner city', *Adoption & Fostering*, 42:4, pp 383–399

Kettle M (2015) *Achieving Effective Supervision*, (IRISS Insight 30) Glasgow: Institute for Research and Innovation and Innovation in Social Services, available at https://www.iriss.org.uk/resources/insights/achieving-effective-supervision

Lawson K and Cann R (2019) *State of the Nation's Foster Care: Full report*, London: Fostering Network

Lynes D and Sitoe A (2019) 'Disenfranchised grief: the emotional impact experienced by foster carers on the cessation of a placement', *Adoption & Fostering*, 43:1, pp 22–34

Manzine J-F and Barsoux J-L (2002) *The Set-Up-To-Fail Syndrome: How good managers cause great people to fail*, Boston: Harvard Business School Press

Miles L (2010) *Holding On and Hanging In: The story of a boy, his foster family and their journey from trauma to healing*, London: CoramBAAF

Morgan N (2013) *Blame My Brain: The amazing teenage brain revealed*, London: Walker Books

Morrison T (1993) *Staff Supervision in Social Care: An action learning approach*, Harlow: Longman

Morrison T (2005) *Staff Supervision in Social Care: Making a real difference for staff and service users*, Brighton: Pavilion Publishing

Morrison T and Wonnacott J (2010) *Supervision Now or Never: Reclaiming reflective supervision on social work*, Haselmere: In-Trac Training and Consultancy, available at https://www.in-trac.co.uk/supervision-now-or-never/

Naish S (2018) *The A–Z of Therapeutic Fostering: Strategies and solutions*, London: Jessica Kingsley Publishers

NSPCC (2020) *Child Sexual Abuse: Learning from case reviews*, London: NSPCC, available at: https://learning.nspcc.org.uk/media/1968/learning-from-case-reviews-child-sexual-abuse.pdf

Octoman O and McLean S (2013) 'Challenging behaviour in foster care: what support do foster carers want?', *Adoption & Fostering*, 38:2, pp 149–158

Odell T (2008) 'Promoting foster carers' strengths: suggestions for strengths-based practice', *Adoption & Fostering*, 32:1, pp 19–28

Ott E, Mc Grath-Lone L, Pinto V, Sanders-Ellis D and Trivedi H (2020) *Mockingbird Programme: Evaluation report*, London: DfE

Ottaway H and Selwyn J (2016) *No-One Told us it was Going to be Like This: Compassion fatigue and foster carers summary report*, Bristol: University of Bristol and Fostering Attachments Ltd

Pallett C, Blackeby K, Bengo C, Yule W, Weissman R, Scott S and Fursland E (2015) *Managing Difficult Behaviour*, London: CoramBAAF

Passmore J (ed) (2010) *Excellence In Coaching: The industry guide*, London: Kogan Page

Plumridge G and Sebba J (2016) *The Impact of Unproven Allegations on Foster Carers*, Oxford: Rees Centre

Ramsay D (1996) 'Recruiting and retaining foster carers: implications for professional practice in Fife', *Adoption & Fostering*, 20:1, pp 42–46

Redfern S, Wood S, Lassri D, Cirasola A, West, G, Austerberry C, Luyten P, Fonagy P and Midgley N (2018) 'The Reflective Fostering Programme: background and development of a new approach', *Adoption & Fostering*, 42:3, pp 234–248

Research In Practice (2014) *07. Leadership and Supervision*, Totnes: Research in Practice, available at: https://fosteringandadoption.rip.org.uk/topics/leadership/

Schofield G and Beek M (2014) *The Secure Base Model: Promoting attachment and resilience in foster care and adoption*, London: CoramBAAF

Schofield G, Cossar J, Ward E, Larsson B and Belderson P (2019) 'Providing a secure base for LGBTQ young people in foster care: the role of foster carers', *Child & Family Social Work*, 24:3, pp 372–381

Sellick C (1996) 'The role of social workers in supporting and developing the work of foster carers', in Hill M (ed) *Signposts in Fostering: Policy, practice and research issues*, London: CoramBAAF

Sidery A (2019) 'Fostering unaccompanied asylum seeking young people: the views of foster carers on their training and support needs', *Adoption & Fostering*, 43:1, pp 6–21

Sinclair I, Gibbs I and Wilson K (2004) *Foster Carers: Why they stay and why they leave*, London: Jessica Kingsley Publishers

Slade J (2012) *Safer Caring: A new approach*, London: Fostering Network

Social Work Reform Board (2010) *Building a Safe and Confident Future: One year on: Proposed standards for employers of social workers in England and proposed supervision framework*, London: Social Work Reform Board, available at: https://assets.publishing.service.gov.uk/government/uploads/system/uploads/attachment_data/file/180798/DFE-00602-2010-3.pdf

Stanley Y (2018) *Supervision and Effective Social Work Practice*, London: Ofsted, available at: https://socialcareinspection.blog.gov.uk/2018/10/23/supervision-and-effective-social-work-practice/

Trafford Safeguarding Children Board (2017) *Serious Case Review: The placements of Child PB*, Stretford: Trafford Safeguarding Children Board

University College London (undated) *Reflective Functioning Questionnaire*, available at: https://www.UCL.ac.uk/psychoanalysis/research/reflective

University of Edinburgh (2017) *Timeline*, Edinburgh: University of Edinburgh, available at: http://www.socialwork.ed.ac.uk/centenary/timeline

Unnamed Local Safeguarding Board (2018) *Serious Case Review: Young Person 'F' (Full Overview Report), Reference 2018/c7320*, London: NSPCC on behalf of an unnamed local safeguarding board

Williams L (2021) *Managing Allegations, Concerns and Complaints against Foster Carers*, London: CoramBAAF

Wonnacott J (2018) *Serious Case Review: Allegations against foster carers and the abuse of children in foster care*, Southampton: Southampton Safeguarding Children Board

Appendix 1
Unannounced visit form

GUIDANCE NOTES FOR COMPLETION OF UNANNOUNCED VISITS

Foster home

It is a requirement of the National Minimum Standards for Foster Care (2011, Standard 10.5) 'that the fostering home is inspected annually, without appointment, by the fostering service to make sure that it continues to meet the needs of foster children'.

Unannounced visit report

Name of carer(s):	
Date of visit:	
Time of visit:	
Visit carried out by:	
People present during the visit	Relationship to foster carer

If the young people in placement were not present, where were they?
If the young person is present, please give their views of the placement.

If the young person has recently had a celebration such as their birthday, please note below any evidence of what they were given.

Health and safety
Please report on the condition of the home. Does it continue to meet the needs of foster child? Is medication stored appropriately? Please check that this is happening. Please also make reference to any specific items around the home that would raise the young people in placement's self-worth, e.g. photos of them in the main living area or certificates they have gained on display.
Young people's bedrooms
Please comment on the condition of the young people's bedrooms, with consideration to the following: Is the room personalised? Is the furniture and decoration appropriate with regard to the age/sex of the young person? Is the condition of the room consistent with the condition of other family rooms? Is the room warm and comfortable? Is the bed, mattress and bedding clean and suitable?
Healthy relationships
Please comment on the presentation of the adults and young people and how they interact, with consideration to the following: Young people's health and self-esteem, the atmosphere in the home, how family members treat each other, any social inequalities. Please include observations regarding the following:

Carer's view on support from the fostering service
Other comments

Name of supervising social worker	
Signed	
Date	

Name of Registered Manager	
Signed	
Date	

Appendix 2
Compassion satisfaction and compassion fatigue (ProQOL) questionnaire

When you *[help]* people you have direct contact with their lives. As you may have found, your compassion for those you *[help]* can affect you in positive and negative ways. Below are some questions about your experiences, both positive and negative, as a *[helper]*. Consider each of the following questions about you and your current work situation. Select the number that honestly reflects how frequently you experienced these things in the *[last 30 days]*.

1 = Never	2 = Rarely	3 = Sometimes	4 = Often	5 = Very often

1	I am happy.	
2	I am preoccupied with more than one person I *[help]*.	
3	I get satisfaction from being able to *[help]* people.	
4	I feel connected to others.	
5	I jump or am startled by unexpected sounds.	
6	I feel invigorated after working with those I *[help]*.	
7	I find it difficult to separate my personal life from my life as a *[helper]*.	
8	I am not as productive at work because I am losing sleep over traumatic experiences of a person I *[help]*.	
9	I think that I might have been affected by the traumatic stress of those I *[help]*.	
10	I feel trapped by my job as a *[helper]*.	
11	Because of my *[helping]*, I have felt "on edge" about various things.	
12	I like my work as a *[helper]*.	
13	I feel depressed because of the traumatic experiences of the people I *[help]*.	

14	I feel as though I am experiencing the trauma of someone I have [helped].	
15	I have beliefs that sustain me.	
16	I am pleased with how I am able to keep up with [helping] techniques and protocols.	
17	I am the person I always wanted to be.	
18	My work makes me feel satisfied.	
19	I feel worn out because of my work as a [helper].	
20	I have happy thoughts and feelings about those I [help] and how I could help them.	
21	I feel overwhelmed because my case [work] load seems endless.	
22	I believe I can make a difference through my work.	
23	I avoid certain activities or situations because they remind me of frightening experiences of the people I [help].	
24	I am proud of what I can do to [help].	
25	As a result of my [helping], I have intrusive, frightening thoughts.	
26	I feel "bogged down" by the system.	
27	I have thoughts that I am a "success" as a [helper].	
28	I can't recall important parts of my work with trauma victims.	
29	I am a very caring person.	
30	I am happy that I chose to do this work.	

[Version 5, 2009]

Reproduced with permission from the publisher.
© B. Hudnall Stamm, 2009. *Professional Quality of Life: Compassion Satisfaction and Fatigue Version 5 (ProQOL)*.

www.isu.edu/~bhstamm or www.proqol.org